The Boy
Behind
the Wall

Poems of Imprisonment and Freedom

By Dalton Harrison

RECONNECTING
RAINBOWS

THE BOY BEHIND THE WALL by Dalton Harrison

Published in the United Kingdom
by Reconnecting Rainbows,
an imprint of Green Spiral Arts

First published in paperback in 2022

ISBN 978-1-8383425-2-4

Printed and bound by Ingram Spark

Reconnecting Rainbows is a collective of transgender and non-binary writers, illustrators, and publishers in the UK and internationally.

For more information, please visit
www.reconnectingrainbows.co.uk

This book is dedicated to the love of my life.
My muse. My best friend. My Bev.
You changed my life.

To
Chapel FM

Sharing Journeys
is so important

Thank you

Dalton

Maybe to understand me
you have to see
my place in history.

- Charles Wright Mills, *The Sociological Imagination*, 1959

Preface

Maybe to understand me, you have to go back to my mother's country in The Netherlands or the effects her parents suffered in the second world war. Or my father, who is very 'British' and only seemed to talk about politics and the Empire and his uncle and father fighting Russians in bars and making a name for themselves. I remember being told I come from a line of boxers and fighters while my mother's side was artists and poets and farmers. All I found was both sides conflicted against the other - which I understood, as I had felt that rage inside myself from the moment I became aware.

I spent thirty-eight years being seen as a woman, living for other people's standards while being abused under their rules as a female and then as a lesbian. I felt lost in unwritten codes of conduct passed down from one generation to the other, while being told there was no such thing as lesbian, bi or transgender people in the eyes of God, and you would 'never have seen this in their time'. My mum tried to console me and tell me over and over that I was a tomboy, nothing more, I would grow out of it - while deep inside, that fear kept me coerced that somehow I was to blame, like a punishment from God. Their narrative grew around me as I became more detached from myself.

Trapped in the stories others told, my eyes hung heavy with guilt and shame as the lies bubbled up inside me over who I really was. I tried to make myself accept the way I was told things simply *were*. I tried not to question, as those questions created anger and more punishment, creating a sense of self-hate.

The day I came out like me, I thought I would be strong; I would be finally free. But coming out as a trans man has left me further still from the community I thought would accept me. I have felt pushed out of the debate on many issues in the LGBTQ+ community and told that my journey in a women's prison is not valid in the discussion on justice for women, as I don't identify. Even if I spent two years inside one, my identity has always been male, but that never stopped someone writing 'female' on my birth certificate and chaining me to a role and perception for most of my life, so it amazes me how people think.

I live in an area marked void, where being a trans man doesn't fit into agencies that only offer support to women who are prison leavers. I wouldn't know their stance on transgender people or if they think someone else deals with them, as none of them came to see me on leaving. The only group who came to talk to me was Through the Gate, and they just said, `I am not sure what your needs are? When do you say you are transgender in prison?' One half want you to prove it, the other half think you want special attention, and the rest think everything you need is performed by some specialist that doesn't seem to exist. I didn't come from a male prison, so why would their support workers cater to me either?

Considering I have been put in a box my whole life, it amazes me now that I am not getting help because they can't find a box to put me in. I have been told I am not vulnerable in council offices after being attacked in several forms of hate crime. I kept going back as it kept happening and tried to get my transgender support group to help. The council panicked enough to let me meet with an LGBTQ support worker, and they gave me a leaflet on hate crime. They told me I needed to go to the police, build up a diary, and start a paper trail. Lucky for me, someone in the office of my private landlord saw an incident and managed to move me three streets down.

But it did not stop. I got chased through the park by five lads when I got off the bus, and I thought right I would do what the council said and ring the hate support line, and when I did, they rang the police on my behalf. I got a call from a victim support officer; the first thing she said was, 'We know you have been inside.' I knew I was not going to get help, and she spent half an hour updating her files, talking about my deadname and talking about me being trans.

But I have jumped too far ahead. Maybe to understand people in prison, you should reflect on them as individuals, rather than a one-size-fits-all justice system of punishment. Leadership makes a clear difference in how we see society and crime, as well as how it is published in the media. Look at Norway and how it deals with the media reports of crime and incarceration and how the importance of rehabilitation is put over punishment alone.

The Prison Reform Trust's statistics such as The Bromley Briefings from 2017 to 2019 reflect the conditions many other people and I faced, highlighting a system that needs more than just reform. I went into prison in 2017; the report shows it was violent, overcrowded with high rates of self-harm. You will see in this book, in the words I have written, what happens behind the context of hard data.

This is continued in the 2018/19 report that highlights how politicians believe we are 'soft on crime' and increased sentences further. How is this reform? How is this protecting the public?

Locking people up for longer in inhuman conditions and then releasing them and expecting them to adapt to society. All I see is the government's gimmicks and voting strategies as they use crime and punishment as a way to sway voters.

I am showing there is a voice behind the locked doors. That people who commit crimes are often victims of crime themselves. That those in the system are not all evil, faceless Netflix true-crime programmes. They are people who are affected by poverty, abuse, addiction, isolation and mental health. People inside the criminal justice system are human, and often their first crime is a mistake that sent them to prison and on a downward spiral. Sometimes it is not even their mistake; it is someone else's, or even a situation that happened because they were born in a high crime area.

These people are suffering horrific conditions outside and then inside. These conditions continue the trauma, and they get out and cannot cope with what they have seen. In some cases, it is so bad outside being in prison is the respite they need. This leaves institutionalization and a revolving door and they continue to repeat the cycle of crime because they have not been shown better but given worse. It makes me think even now of all those I know who have died when they got out from suicide, drugs or being beaten to death by their partners.

Maybe now's the time we all need to join together to change a view that's clearly not working or at the very least consider the impact of throwing money into building more prisons when what you already have is a system full of people who mostly have been impacted by special measure school systems, lack of community support, poverty, class, domestic abuse, trauma, lack of privilege, mental health and racism. We need to look at school state systems and how they are used as a dumping ground for those that will eventually fall down the next step to prison.

Broken systems and structures are nothing more than giant human waste recycling plants, a spin cycle wash for many generations of families expected to teach the next generation. When they have not been taught themselves, the system generates wealth for some and pain for others. The news follows a crime story; then the media connects the rest to sell more papers. The politicians grab a chance to sway voters on 'tough on crime' policies, then click baiters step in and the advertisers cash in as they are sharing these crime stories on social media attached to their adverts. People are turned into an evil pantomime figure, not someone who has mental health issues, needs medication, is homeless or is suffering from PTSD. We share regardless. Netflix picks up the trend, brings us more true-life crime programmes and competes with Prime for the rights.

Society condemns those caught in the system forever by being just a google away from failure and shame; this is the new style of public hanging online. Just the playthings of society, the comment section for trolls to feed off. Stopped from getting a chance in the future from companies and bosses searching online before accepting someone for that job. When does someone become a criminal that does not deserve a second chance? When does someone who needs help stop being a person at all and no longer be thought of in the context of an individual, a father, mother, brother? When do we no longer view that person as a person? Not a label, not a crime, a headline? When does a system take a child from a problem to a criminal and set them down like nothing else?

Not every child has the same experiences as others; they have not had the sights and sounds that enable them to grow - or perhaps it is provided through a lens that perhaps hasn't been changed in generations. I remember doing a Christmas Panto when I was still inside prison, and the reaction we got inside was amazing. One girl came up to us the last year we performed and said she didn't know what a panto was but came because it got her off the wing, and she had never had seen anything like it in her life; she was in her twenties. I am not saying crime should go unpunished, but I am questioning why a girl barely out of her teens is crying in prison because she just never knew there was such a thing as a panto, and it made her Christmas.

We need to start having these conversations. Debating what kind of society we are, if we say we are a better generation than before. Why are we not looking at the prison system as a structure that is running side by side, a society that is a community that needs support, that prison is a subculture that is creating new members every day? Maybe next time we march for a revolution, we start thinking first, is that not what revolutions are? Changing how we feel as a society. Laws change all the time and how it affects the generation that follows is how some generations improve or come unstuck. Imagine if some laws never made it to the bill, where we would be now? Such as The Sexual Offences Act 1967 or Section 28, the Equality Act, abortion being made legal in Northern Ireland, or the end of free TV licences for people over seventy-five. Do we stand up for every change or protest about what we don't agree with, or do we look at what they mean to us as a society?

Yet, these protests never stretch inside the prison system. I wonder if George Floyd had died in prison rather than while being arrested if we would have gotten to the same place? Or if Patsy Stevenson had been treated like that for voicing her opinion while in prison and handcuffed and lifted by officers to the segregation unit, rather than at a protest where people had taken pictures, would we be having the same debate about safety for women and ending violence against women? I have seen a 5ft, 18-year-old girl who looked like she could be a model, with piercing blue eyes and an oval shaped face. I looked down in shock at her purple torso as she wore a vest and below a pair of shorts showed a perfect size 11 boot imprint on her inside thigh. Having been in the police cells a few nights before, she came out of her cell and was sent back to change as she had broken the decency policy of the prison.

When will protests start about the Government building 500 more prisons for women and start reinvesting in community support instead? When will we shout that we don't want families to be torn apart and children to face care? With most women facing a sentence of six months or less, all prison does is punish - there is no justice in leaving them homeless, childless and jobless.

At the very least, we need to start closing the gap between the best and worst prisons. We need to realise what has been done so far is not working. Was it right anyway when we can look back in history, what the system has done to so many people and to generations of families? Why do we continue to repeat the same questions and wonder why we have a high level of recidivism? Why are we still accepting the Government's answer to these problems within the prison system by letting them say on our behalf the answer is still longer sentencing and more prisons to house all these criminals?

To me prison is just an extension of the old-style Victorian workhouse that serves no purpose in modern society but to punish and is used to throw people in who can't be dealt with in a mental health system that has been destroyed by years of lack of funding. Why as a society do we only believe people are either good or bad? Why are we not talking about how people get institutionalized so quickly when they have come from unstructured and overcrowded areas of deprivation and often have backgrounds so traumatized that they may thrive on the structure? That when they are released back into the chaos, prison may look like a better option?

But I am not saying anything academics and prison reform advocates don't already know, but what little's being done about these matters reflects another level of privilege that allows people to hide behind the mask of justice and law and order. If the future is ever going to change, we have to listen and learn from the past. We have to imagine a new reality, a new society that does not think it's acceptable to let new-born babies die in prison and to clap when human beings kill themselves just because they are deemed criminal.

To foster change and find humanity and evolve as a society we have to explore why it's based in hate in the first place. When I say based in hate there was a time when everyone in society accepted slavery, each time in history a whole group of people were treated like they were not even human, like the fallen women of the Victorian era, or that the suffragettes faced force feeding and torture. Oscar Wilde, Alan Turing and others were punished by laws that said they were evil - yet where would we be today without their input in society at the time they were hated?

My thoughts go back to all the people society has accepted back into mainstream culture that were once deemed criminal by the law of that time, such as Martin Luther King Jr, Bill Gates, Frank Sinatra, Jay-Z, Eminem, David Bowie, Keanu Reeves, Elvis Presley, Bruno Mars, Mick jagger, Cher. If we had signed all these people off for the crimes they committed, the world would not have been the same, so why can we not lift that level of forgiveness to a few more people? I know I am one of the lucky ones, no matter how hard it was I did manage to get pulled up by someone just before I was ready to give up, but even so I know now I could have still gone two ways once I was trapped within the justice system. I found my sense of reality began changing very quickly once inside. Doubt set in, as my own perception of reality was questioned daily. Being locked inside what is simply another world with people who often need medical help, not locking up - that creates fantasies, as one reality is blurred and seems to implode on itself as new and old people enter back inside. There were so many different levels of perceptions that blended together and you were left wondering what was real.

I saw three violent suicide attempts in the first few weeks alone. Three women from different races and ages. What makes someone just out of their teens want to do that? Or one who is in their thirties thinks there is no other option but to throw herself off a fire exit off the second floor? Or how a black woman can still be seen as aggressive even when she says `I am going to jump'? When I heard the alarms go off and an officer in charge replied: 'Let her jump. The worst she can do' is break her legs.' I felt myself die a little more inside. I saw fights and bullying. I felt trapped, like every option that was left inside prison was not making sense but it was the only way we were told to behave.

This discourse community was run by officers and created by Governors where prisoners had to survive, not only in the hierarchy of staff structures, but against each other and the prisoner pecking order. I am not saying all prison officers or staff are bad, but how can the few that are good work in a system that leaves them with no time to do what is really needed? I have had officers help me and then two minutes later other officers do the exact opposite. I have seen officers treat some prisoners better not because of their crime but because they are tough, and those officers continue to shout at those who are scared and vulnerable. In any job the stress can become too much and some officers who help out others are frowned on by those in power and put on the worst duties or given warnings for not completing work quick enough, as they were trying to do extra by supporting those who need it. There are several officers that I wish I could have met on the outside, but on the inside as an officer I couldn't have asked for better with what they were given.

As an individual prisoner it was impossible - you had to create a family inside or risk having to fight and miss out on so many opportunities, which could be anything from food, clothes, stamps to write home or just getting by on the exercise yard. Once you find your place you just have to accept the way it is, but what do you do when violence and survival become the norm? What do you do when it's time for you to get out? The world runs differently to how prison life works, not just physically but emotionally. I was able to take so many opportunities that are no longer available now in covid times, yet it amazes me how I read how the prisons want to keep the regime and keep saying it was working.

To create change you have to be the change; to be the change you have to change the way it is. Why are we not fighting as a society to change the system or at least to be more in line with Norway? Some people say it would never work, but it does; how can humanity over punishment not work? Norway has incredible programmes to aid with rehabilitation and focus on training and education as well as creativity and mindfulness.

What little we had in the female prison in resources and education, I took and used, and it helped - and those that did the same as me are doing far better now than those who didn't. I did everything I could, but it was not made easy for me and those who tried along with me. I took rehabilitative courses such as TSP which is a thinking skills programme. I was an orderly, a mentor, a diversity rep, a listener (trained by the Samaritans), a Shannon Trust mentor, a 'red band' that could go unsupervised and work in the prison gardens in areas no other prisoners were allowed to go. I took classes and started going into higher education with the Durham University 'Inside Out' project as well as the pioneering work of Dr Phil Heron - 'Think like a Scientist' course – and with support from Prisoners Education Trust, I passed my access course in Arts and Languages with The Open University.

Even after all that, the prison regime makes it hard to access study groups or get computer time, even a quiet place to study, let alone getting work books on time and DVDs as you cannot access the internet and you have to wait for paperwork to be cleared and passed through security - that's even if you can access a DVD player, as you have to buy your own - and you also have to be an 'enhanced' prisoner, I was lucky my partner had all those things at the time.

There are so many other problems you can face inside prison such as competing for funding, not only that but resources, and the male estate clearly has better support and funding than any female estate I was in. Jobs as well as courses in female prisons are often very gendered. When I asked what training I could do, I could either work in hair and beauty, sew or clean! There were other options, but nowhere near the standard in the men's prisons. We found out about those from men who were writing to their girlfriends about what they could access in their prisons, as couples often got locked up in different prisons at the same time.

Not only that, but prison education is based on a particular type of prisoner - for instance, those who can't read at all, or at the lowest level. Those who come into prison with a higher education often find themselves mentoring, with no other options to see them progress, and for long-term prisoners that can lead to a sense of depression as they find there is nothing that they can do to give them purpose.

The overall regime inside prison often saw me spending days locked in my cell in unbearable heat, while not seeing loved ones for weeks or showering in days, until I was able to get on a better wing - which so many are not lucky enough to achieve. Even then we had often gone without running water and had to share toilets that could not be flushed, while other wings often reported unclean water coming through the pipes which I often thought was because the prisons need to be upkept better with electric plugs giving out shocks or blowing up. There never seemed to be any worry over the public finding out about these problems - but if there was a special event, it would often be said, 'We don't want you to have too much fun - what would the public say?'

Mental health waiting times mean that some people will never be trusted enough to be on such a wing as I had managed to get on, regardless of how good their behaviour is, because of the fear that desperation would lead to some paperwork. I still had to fight to keep my place, as when my mother died I was as good as told if I didn't appear like I was dealing with it I would be moved off my wing, as they couldn't watch me all the time. There were many people who got moved off the enhanced wing for crying too much or being emotional. Medications could play a part in what happens to you inside as well as what you can access in prison, and those put on meth (the prison uses this drug for most addiction problems, one-size-fits-all approach) will be controlled by this drug until they are released, unable to deal with anything else.

But none of the staff shortage bang up culture of that time can ever be compared to a new dawn that shut the prison system down: COVID-19. That put a stop to education and association, from families meeting on visits to mental health appointments, and kept people in their cells for as close to 24 hours as possible. But the real question that lingers in my mind is this: if COVID can change the prison system so quickly by shutting it down, and then developing technology that was said to never work in prison - such as Purple Visits, a digital system that allows prisoners and families to visit online like a Zoom call, which is a miracle given the normal paper-based mindset of prisons that reminds me of a pre-Internet era - why can't a fairer, more humane system be introduced when restrictions begin to ease inside? Why does change need to be forced by bad things and never be used for better?

This collection of my poetry is my own narrative, my identity and my journey - it evolved as I grew. It shows my time in the prison system and the effects that the system can have on you. But above al,l it shows an individual behind government census and headlines and 'in the public's best interest' comments and justifications of a trolling culture. It strips down data to show an emotive energy of desperation, pain, but also hope and survival. A reflection of life inside and out that shows if you live long enough you will be many things within that life, a child, a woman, a man, a victim, a daughter, a bully, a son, a hero, a villain, an underdog, a winner, an activist, a writer and a poet, an artist, a friend, an enemy and teacher, a student and mentor and if you're truly lucky your get to learn from your mistakes and be able to show it is possible to others who cannot see that far ahead yet, that they can move on.

For me I have so far lived a life in hindsight not knowing anything further than my own social and economic bias bubble. My life was a filter that I didn't release was destroying me and those around me. In prison I lost everything but found education and above all love when I met my partner who I am still with now. Even with her support I struggled with the dark path the prison can lead you down, and with mental health and hopelessness, with limited resources that can mean the difference between an officer taking the time and not having the time to support you left down to their own personal choice.

In prison you have to survive day to day, but I never realized the true horror was waiting on the days to my own release day. That I would find a probation system and a society that cared more about the crime then they did about what was happening to people. Public attitudes and what peaks their attention is trapped within a loop of glamorizing crime and judging those in a bias that has been passed down by politicians and laws that prey on social exclusion, a system that starts from birth, in strict views on race, gender and education systems that still practice off-rolling. Is justice that simple, if statistics show which percentage of the population are more likely than others to go to prison? There are many exceptions to this theory, but even so, can we truly believe in everything we have been told?

Since I have got out, I have been shunned while looking for housing. I have been stopped from accessing education because of ID issues and other undisclosed reasons. I have got accepted for jobs and then when I have declared, 'I need to disclose a criminal conviction', they put the phone down or stop emailing and that is before I can even say for what. I have tried, failed and succeeded in time to do it all again. I have worked with criminal justice classes in universities in Durham and had my poetry used in Bradford and Leeds universities.

I have performed a play in prison that was written and based on experiences of inside, and built a collective of like-minded people I had named Standfast which is a reference to when I first went into prison and was sweeping the floor when the officer first shouted,

'There is a standfast!' and I stood frozen in mid-sweep as they asked me what I was doing, and I said, 'I am standing fast.' They told me I was an idiot and to go to the office where we would be counted, and that standfast meant a prisoner was lost, so we had to check the count was right and re-count everyone.

I keep moving forward no matter what and I often got knocked down quicker than I could get up. When I did secure a job regardless of a criminal conviction, I ended up losing it when COVID hit. But like many, I feel the shame of being seen in each newspaper or gossip magazine I pass reporting how criminals are the scum of the earth. Social media sharing posts of people I recognized, saying 'This person is in your area, we need to get them out!' - and I receive friend requests from people who were in for drugs, assault, shoplifting or robbery, using their middle names for fear of a backlash.

But even in all this I have also had many individuals act purely out of kindness that has solely got me through my first year out. From a sweet couple in a train station who saw me with too many prison bags, struggling to find the taxi rank. To the taxi driver who asked me, 'Why do you want to go *there*?' - in reference to the bail hostel address I gave him - who just knew he should keep his mouth shut after I said, 'Because they told me to.' To Jane at the Jobcentre who got me through every appointment with a smile and let me sit there waiting for a moment she had free in between appointments when I turned up randomly to ask questions - and above all I'm grateful to her for not sanctioning me when I missed an appointment, as I nearly got recalled to prison for signing a lease without the formal 'yes' from probation. I was so scared of being homeless, I agreed to the only place that offered me a six-month lease. Of course I left voicemails and texts telling them what I was going to do, but they disappeared when I signed the paperwork and they told me I was in breach of my licence conditions. I felt defeated that week, waiting for a knock at the door from the police or at best a warning. I had seen so many others that had simply broken probation rules, not committed new offences after release, and they mostly thought 'fuck it!' and ended up doing something worse and getting recalled anyway.

After that setback I came back in full force continuing what I loved, and that was learning and talking about prison reform, which took me to Durham University, Milton Keynes Open University campus and the BBC Broadcast in London. I had the privilege to work with The Inside-Out prison exchange programme, The Prison Education Trust and Dr Phil Heron - Think like a Scientist. With a quiet resolve I had started in prison I continued to be the change I wanted to see. I just kept going and kept moving forward no matter what was happening around me. I went to LGBTQ book clubs. I went to transgender support groups. I marched in my first pride parade. I started Standfast, a poetry and performance collective. I attended writing groups at Swarthmore college with the most amazing teacher, writer and mentor Gill Lambert, as well as Becky Cherriman whose incredible poetry moved me to want to keep going and took me to another world. Not only inspiring me with the power of her words but making me believe I could achieve more than I ever dreamed, such as wanting to go to University.

Becky was the kind of teacher that made you look at things differently and start to pay attention. She took classes in art and writing at the hostel I was in, and after my first lesson I knew I was hooked. These voices carried me, they guided me to re shape and rework what there was and taught me that the power of words can create anything. When I was still in the hostel, I worked with Opera North on their community lullaby workshop. On leaving the hostel my surroundings were bleak, but with the support of Emma, Pam and Jackie who worked in the hostel, I continued to pop into writing groups at the hostel and felt myself grow in confidence chatting to Christine and Vinny who worked there and always made me feel I was supported. I went back to HMP Newhall to do a talk on what it is like to live in a hostel with Emma the manager and I managed to put some of my own demons to rest in the process.

I built up Standfast and the first play *High Risk* was performed in The Holbeck and raised money for Ripon House Hostel. I also got my dream of being on the front cover of *Inside Time* magazine. I continued talking on the radio, did a video for Inside Prison on education, and was in a metro article about the importance of prison education. I wrote for *Inside Time* and *Pink news* on what it was like being a transgender man in prison. I continued even in lockdown with poetry events and wrote an article called 'All there is, is you' about suffering bereavement in prison for Sister Magazine X TGN. Each goal led me to a new one, like when Ben Leapman, a writer for *Inside Time* asked me a trivia question in an email: 'What has been achieved in 2020 by only four people: POA chairman Steve Gillan, IAP chair Juliet Lyon, Prison Service chief exec Jo Farrar, and yourself?' I didn't know how I could be linked with professionals who had shaped my very existence months before and how I lived in prison. He replied that we are all the only people to have a picture twice on the front cover of *Inside Time* in 2020.

I have done so many exciting things and I don't want to write them all down, but one question that sticks in my mind that comes up when I do radio or podcasts is: If I could see any positive changes in the prison system what would they be? I think that across the board, mentoring programs should be given more importance. Peer mentor work is unvalued and we should be using the wealth of knowledge of those who have the skills to help others and who have been there. Training people in prison to be peer mentors will not only help those coming in to see a light at the end of the tunnel, but also pick up where the officers are not reaching, whether it's lack of time, lack of patience, or lack of training.

In my time I saw a dedicated few officers get stressed and messed about by the system they were enforcing by trying to support people in a way that should be mandatory. This way, at least they could be supported by mentors, or at the very least have it recognized within the system that what they do is valid by supporting prisoners above just the usual role of prison officer. Also if peer mentoring is developed inside prison, then this could lead to a job on the outside - which will support people on coming out but also teach them that working hard pays off, as the jobs I worked hard at for two years meant nothing when I got out. Maybe that can change with schemes such as these.

Peer mentor roles that lead to work on the outside can help bridge the gap between the officers and prisoners, and also aid the officers with the stress they get from prisoners who need more and constantly ask for help. I saw this many times inside. One such incident was an outburst from one of the old-school officers. I was in a class with Durham Inside Out, talking about officers and prisoners, and one officer who had to sit in due to being with a restricted-status prisoner began shouting over our conversation and said, 'You expect me to be a mother, a mental health worker, a friend, a doctor, the bloody lot. I am here to do my job. I am a prison officer, I have the keys, that's it. The job has changed so much over the years but the training hasn't, what about our needs?'

I felt her pain but I also felt my own, when all you see is the same faces every day and no real contact with the outside world – and for some people, none, if they don't have family or friends. An officer is all you have on a daily basis, and trying to get an appointment for healthcare and support anywhere else is near impossible half the time.

I have also seen chaplaincy deal with things that an officer or a mental health support worker should be dedicating a full-time job to. There are so many people picking up or dropping real lives in a system that is not fit for purpose.

Peer mentoring inside can develop confidence and skills in the mentor that can be used as a job on the outside, which shows there is hope to rebuild lives if you put the work in - not just working your socks off, sewing for a sentence, then getting out to find no one wants to hire you. Creating peer mentoring jobs inside to develop outside can be a great asset to those in the field already that are experiencing lack of resources and time issues as case overload leaving many to slip through the cracks. The fields where peer mentoring could be used include mental health support, drugs and alcohol recovery, housing and homelessness, LGBTQ support, and probation support.

That brings me back to prisons and the policymakers who need to just stop saying they are dealing with issues such as education, rehabilitation and overcrowding, and just get on with it already. That does not mean make new prisons, it means improve the old ones, update what you have, and bridge the gap in resources from male prisons to female prisons. The divide between male and female wages in prison and what they can access is horrific. I will never stop saying make education a must, not a luxury, and stop blocking education resources that are trying to support prisoners by security red tape. Security in prison says that digital cannot work - yet look how they moved online visits into prison when they were pushed! There are security cleared laptops that are not being allowed into prison, people not being able to access education - and that again is highlighting the flaws of a system that wants to punish, not change, those in it. Unless pushed by society, this will not change, but remain the same.

Those on degrees should be supported, and I don't mean given special treatment, but they don't get even 2% of the support I get as an outside student. The women's prisons are the worst: having seen what male prisons have, I am shocked by the difference. It is not good enough to say it is 'just the way it is'. Protecting women should not just be reserved for protests, what happens to women is more than violence by police, men or society; it is institutionally ground into the prison system. I was one of the lucky ones, I went into prison with mental health problems but those problems did not involve addiction or underlying health problems and I did not get thrown a dose of medication to control my sentence, although I nearly drank a full dose of methadone thinking it was Night Nurse when I asked the nurse for antihistamines. The nurse only told me to give it back after I repeatedly said I was usually given tablets and questioned what I was being given, where everyone else was just doing what they were told. My last name was similar to another prisoner on a high dose of methadone and that was enough for the mix-up. It was also enough for the mistake to be made more than once, as someone else I know ended up taking it and not recovering for a long time.

Each journey is different. My journey was met with so many obstacles, but I still had the desire and the strength to move forward. So many people in the system had that kicked out of them at school, by their family, partner or living in extreme poverty, and others because of their race, religion or colour. I found strength and hope by falling in love inside with a wonderful woman I am still with. I found a way to evolve inside an environment that destroys you, by using art, performance and poetry and education as a way to recover my life. This focus kept me alive long enough so I could turn my life around. For so many others, they just go back inside because their prison family is all they have. But like I said, it could have gone either way, because once you fall into the rabbit hole it's hard to see your way back out.

I sit, my back numb on the cold stone wall. My hands are shaking. My head seems caught between now and then.

It's 2017. My eyes scan a letter.

All I could see was my life from a baby to now. Was this all I was now? A series of boxes to be filled. Mistakes made. I was not asking to be painted as the victim, but I was scared I was falling into sounding full of self-pity.

I had grown up without ever seeing me in any representation. No-one but those around me showed me the way - and the way they showed me, showed me I was born wrong. I learned to hide, to feel the guilt of me like a chain around my neck, to give up before I began because I was not enough. The strict religious hand of my father's side and the guilt of my mother's.

Violence never appears overnight; it grows like a seed in a family setting. For children it may not even be noticed - as what is the norm, or a safe space when there is nothing to be compared to? But when the violence increases dramatically, the perspective of that child begins to change. It did for me the day my father smashed a glass against the living room table and put it up to my mother's throat. I know now we were both victims and had been for a long time and no law had ever come to our rescue. The court told me I was nearly 16 and an adult. I was not protected and was left with my father. In the years that followed, no one who attacked me physically or mentally got sentenced.

I learned to survive. I had to just carry on. I had to adapt. Environmental dependency and compartmentalisation was now my life, I knew what was expected of me, even before I understood what coercive control was. I knew if I was good, If I did what I was told, I did not get hit.

I was now labelled a criminal but that was not based in the framework of my upbringing. But in the Law of now, the stamp of justice had been printed on my paperwork. I was now a file. Blame. Judge. Jury. Guilty. Sentence. Branded. My mind fights back, still unable to deal with the past. Defined and linked to only my worst mistakes.

There was no newspaper article when I was a security guard and ran back toward the fire and the ammonia plant next to it as there was a man sleeping in his wagon and I had to get him to safety. No, my boss called me stupid and started to investigate my actions and accused me of setting the fire, until a faulty machine was found as the starting point. The fire brigade said five more minutes and there would have been no factory left if I had not been there.

There was no news slot for me when I worked in a care home and a resident began choking on her dinner and the supervisors stood by and told her to drink some water as she turned blue and her head went into her plate. I ran round the serving hatch and gave her the Heimlich Manoeuvre. I was looked at like I had broken the rules, as paperwork needed doing and questions would be asked.

My cell banged my eyes and my letter came back into focus, it was from my solicitors. 'For the offence of Assault Occasioning Actual Bodily Harm, you were both found guilty.' I close my eyes. 'Immediate imprisonment.' I heard a shout out the window and a cell door bang, I jumped like a recoiling spring as the system seemed to welcome me in. I read further: 'I enclose a Client Feedback Questionnaire and would be obliged if you would kindly complete and return it to me at your convenience.'

I did not know who I was anymore. All the things I thought were me were now being put in a skip I had hired only a month before, outside the house I used to think was my home. How do I go from adversity to worrying about bills or my job - to this? My life had so much purpose and now all I saw was graffiti on my wall. Where do I find resilience in what looks like the gateway between earth and hell? Locked doors. Heat. Stale air. Bars on windows facing barbed wire and concrete. Walls. Screaming. Pale skin. Lines everywhere. Waiting. Standing. Sitting. Self-harm. Hungry. Trapped. Controlled. Isolated. A captive in a culture I could not understand with its hidden rules and language.

The cell door flung back. I saw the side of a pregnant woman who was in for benefit fraud, rubbing her belly, looking down the landing at all the cells. The black and white figures moved around her in a blur and the glint of keys vanished. I questioned how the stress of this place would affect her or even be passed down to her child. She turned and smiled as she saw me, still pressed up against the wall that my bed was secured to. I did not want pity. I wanted to be told where I could find salvation. Hope. My file now had me as a picture next to Violent Criminal, how could I move on? I could never forgive myself, but would I find forgiveness anywhere else? I wanted to disown my past but maybe the real problem was, would it ever disown me?

Ten Minutes

Characters
KATIE is the girl in prison: she is in her thirties, tall, stocky, hair tied back in a tight ponytail, dark brown hair with brown eyes.

VICKY is the girl in the living room: in her thirties, tall with long blonde hair and blue eyes, has her hair down.

Setting
Modern day. Split stage.
One side shows a living room with a few chairs and a sofa. There's a landline phone on a small table.
The other side shows a room with a phone mounted on the wall.

TEN MINUTES
The light comes up on the split stage. We hear the ringing of a phone. KATIE stands next to the wall-mounted phone, waiting for it to connect. With white knuckles and her other hand touching the wall, she appears stressed and paranoid.

VICKY enters the living room and picks up the landline phone. She is anxious and excited.

KATIE: Hello, hello? Vicky are you there? Thank God it connected! This has been the longest week of my life, please tell me you're alright! (*Her fingers coil round the receiver, hot with the fingers of so many before her, she plays with the wire as her eyes dart back and forth*)

VICKY: Katie! Are you ok? I've been sick with worry, it's been hell here! I don't know what to say. He found out one of your letters, he saw, he's been acting weird since you went in, he saw the headlines and bought the paper just so he could slam it on the kitchen counter and give me the look and lecture in his big "I am" voice. He was livid, shouting, "This is your friend, you had her round my house, did you fuck her? What rooms did you fuck her in? Our lounge? Our bed? Under our wedding pictures in the car?"

KATIE: Shit, the letter, he got the letter? Not the last one, not the one when I was remembering our last night! On the sofa together? (*she gasps*)

VICKY: He found the box. I keep it hidden. He never lifted a finger for years now he suddenly finds it and the money my dad gave me. I was saving it to leave him, I didn't want him to see it, couldn't put it in the bank, he called me every name under the sun (*she sobs*)

KATIE: Did he hurt you? (*Raises voice*) I swear if he hurts you I will....

VICKY: (*pleading*) Don't, please! I hit him first, he just slapped me...

KATIE: (*spitting through gritted teeth*) I feel sick, I feel so helpless, I want to hit him!

VICKY: (*whispering*) Stop, stop, don't say anymore, the line's clicking.

KATIE: I know, I know. They'll probably cut us off. I love you. I can't breathe. I thought I would never talk to you again, I thought that was it, it was over, you were gone...(*she trails off*)

VICKY: (*becoming angry*) You are the one that left, I'm the one that's left to pick up the pieces, arguing with people at work defending you, they all know we're together. She told them all at work, she read your phone when you stayed with her.

KATIE: (*barking*) Gillian did what?!

VICKY: (*growling*) Yes, you slept over that last week before you went inside. While you slept, she read your phone - didn't take long to figure out the texts were from me, even though you changed the name. Once she thought about it, and she put two and two together, she called me a homewrecker, me! Said you and her were going to move in together, she was getting a flat so you could be together. Said she loves you, said I was a greedy whore, that I had a family. I was married, I had someone - she didn't have anyone and that I am greedy. Why did you go to her? You know she's always liked you!

KATIE: I had no choice, I couldn't exactly go to yours and stay over. I had nowhere to go, no one to help, no money. Me and Jade had split up, but I was stuck living with her. She took it all, I was completely trapped. You have no idea what it was like! *(she breaks off)*

VICKY: You don't either, he says he is going to destroy me, why am I always the bad guy, with Gillian getting everyone on her side at work, with him and his family!

KATIE: I think we established I am the bad guy! I am sorry for Gillian, I am sorry for Jade, I'm sorry I just got with you and now I am here. I am sorry for mucking about with Gillian, but she was there - she helped me and I can't take that away from her. She fed me, saw me, sheltered me when Jade kicked me out and I know it's messed up. I know it doesn't make it right how I acted or what I did, but I just felt so out of control. My life was on fire and I was running around trying to blow it out, but spreading the goddamn flames! I never dreamed for a second you would love me, I never thought for a minute we could be more than a stolen night, more than lingering thoughts and wishes and hopes and daydreams. You have always been untouchable, you think even before my marriage ended I didn't think "wow" every time I looked at you? That I didn't hover between shifts and try to act like I was there early for no apparent reason, or late because I forgot something. It was always you. (*She whimpers*)

VICKY: This isn't always about you! The second I saw you all those years ago - you came in for your interview and I caught a look at you. I was working days back then and you just walked in on hot air with a swagger I had never seen before - all cheeky grins and wide eyed looks around. I knew then you were gonna be trouble. I knew then, even then, in that second of you being behind that door and me not knowing you, to you being there and me wanting and waiting and thinking, you were going to get me in trouble. I just knew my life was never gonna be the same again. God I just wish I had been different, I never should have mucked you around. I never should've let you feel I was playing power games...

KATIE: *(shocked)* What do you mean?

VICKY: When I said I liked you but my life was complicated…

KATIE: *(butting in)* And I said so was mine!

VICKY: Yeah, but after that night at work and then the day you first came round and I called it off before it started. I said I couldn't do it. I shouldn't have invited you round, I should not have messed with your head…

KATIE: And then I kissed you.

KATIE, her back against the wall, looks up, holding the phone receiver and smiles.

VICKY: But after that at work I saw all the times you looked at me and I never returned your gaze. When you messaged me and I saw it was you, but always waited, I always left you hanging. Then I called it off again and that night at bonfire night I saw you turn up, I saw you look for me because I said I'd be there and when you finally saw me I made out like I was busy having fun. But I fed off your energy, your need, your lust and want of me. I felt it no matter how far away you were. It excited me.

KATIE: *(trying to cut her off)* Look, stop, it's OK, please…

VICKY: Maybe you would not have run to Gillian. *(she chokes)*

KATIE: *(softly)* All I know is I love you.

VICKY: What's that noise?

VICKY leans forward, her eyes getting bigger.

KATIE: Something going on, everyone running about. I hate this place, it's mental. I don't get what's happening in here half the time. It's like being in a foreign country.

The noise becomes too loud to hear her.

KATIE: *(shouting)* From the second I got in here it's been like a Mad Max movie. How can I see what I have seen and come out the same person I went in?

The noise gets worse.

VICKY: What is it, Kate? Are you there? Hello! Kate! Don't ring till I send you a letter about what's happening Kate, I will need time to sort him. I don't want to give him any more ammunition.

KATIE: I gotta go, there's legs, legs hanging over the landing, if they jump they'll land on me. God, the alarms, they're coming!

The phone cuts off. The screen goes black and the light is solely on the living room.

VICKY is left holding the receiver to her ear and puts it slowly down, while moving her hand to her face. She begins to sob, then we hear the dial tone.

PHONE O/S: Please hang up and try again. Please hang up and try again.

The lights cut to black.

CURTAIN

One Person, One Wall, One Prison

Characters

JONES, a prisoner in her late thirties with short blonde hair. She's womanly and solid, but slender. Blue eyes and dark eyebrows, contrasting to her hair.

FEMALE OFFICER, never seen on stage.

Setting

A prison cell in the north of England. Present day.

ONE PERSON, ONE WALL, ONE PRISON

Very dim light comes up, we can just make out a prison cell. We can't see who's speaking, just hear their voice. It's Jones, talking to the wall.

JONES: How long has it been, me and you! You have seen the worst of me here - the snot, the vile tongue of hate, then despair. The one thing I have! You! Who echoes my dreams every night? You keep me warm when outside is nothing but flashing thunder like my heart, like the night sky. Lonely, controlled, forgotten.

You don't forget, you see me, you listen when the door shuts with a bang and keeps me here.

Minute falling over minutes like atoms taking shape. Hour over hour – each hurdle bigger than the last. For what? To reach the end, to win! There is no trophy, no gold medal for me.

Day follows day like the lines in dinner queues, then to medicate one by one. 90% of us are on antidepressants, need I say more? Counting the birds on the roof tops is like counting the years that have passed.

But you, you are solid. You know my voice, like I know every scar you have from all those who have been with you, every scratch, mark, burn, line, I see! I see. We are in this together, my friend.

The dark room begins to get light, a speck in the corner getting bigger till it turns into a spotlight and you realise a woman (Jones) is sitting in bed in a cell. The light is coming through bars and she pats the wall and laughs.

JONES: No one would believe you, you know what I told you, what's happened over these years between us, too many to think on, not enough yet to feel blessed: a few more hurdles, ay well, just a few more...

In the distance the sound of keys and footsteps coming closer, shouting getting nearer.

OFFICER (offstage): Come on, Jones, wake up! (*sound of unlocking*) Morning! (*sound of unlocking*) Make yourself decent!

Jones is moving round the room as steps get closer, the spotlight is on the sink. The sound stops, she looks up, hunched over the small sink, turning to the side she stands up straight. We hear the sound of keys.

She walks offstage, the single spotlight gets bigger and lights up the cell and we can see a bed, wall, barred window and memory board full of pictures and letters. A paper rose is on a small light-coloured pine desk under the window with a notepad in it and pen.

JONES: Well, well, I am back, bet it wasn't too quiet with me gone. I see they have done room checks! The sun was shining, it felt so good, could you see it? Did it shine for you? I was walking down the long corridor, they walked me from the overnight wing back here. The sun was beaming through each bar, like the grill in a cooker, but I felt different.

I heard someone hum JP Cooper's September Song as I walked further. I heard a door unlock and an officer was singing it as they walked up. Someone walked down humming the chorus, then others did! Singing the words, like they were taken over all unaware but joining in one collective choir!

I felt alive, like the sun. From each window lay a platform for me to glide straight up to you, Wall, to tell you that I can breathe like someone opened a window and let me see out. Over more than just grey and chairs and floodlights and wire and fences and the floors of buildings folded shut like a flat pack. I felt myself stood at the foot of a hill and below me was grass and sand, then sea. I told you about the sea, the rolling waves of freedom - wet and deep and infinite. I told you, Wall, about the horizon that doesn't stop at a locked door. The sky that rides out like wild horses in that film that repeats on Channel Four. You know, Wall!

Don't hold back, you know! When I told you I wanted more, when you just looked back at me and showed me shapes and shadows of peaks and valleys, but I wanted to taste the salt! Feel the breeze! I wanted to run through texture that wasn't sticky laminate flooring or threaded thin carpet. You just showed me a blank white canvas. You can't see what I do! There's no movie reel in your head to holiday romances, too young to worry and too old to hold back!

It's true, old friend! We only regard the missed kisses, the lost moments that took form, but never reached a solid shape! I said, "How will I have this more times than we have talked, again!" As if being stuck with a thousand women and no chance of a man walking into my life isn't bad enough! One that can give me a smile and remind me I am the girl. I want to be that girl! I want him to look and want to look at me instead of the sunset.

What's the use in dreaming? I have had my hair pulled by many women, but when you want that September song, what then?

Maybe I want it all, maybe there's nothing past you, Wall, but something without shape. But I have never felt like this - or have I, did I forget?

I went into Inductions and saw all the new prisoners, ready for induction and as I was about to start, there at the doorway - tall, thick set. And I stopped still. My minutes changed from fluid to solid and I took a breath.

I didn't think I needed that, I haven't taken in such a breath in all the years it took me to get here. Maybe the last time was at the dock when they said 'Guilty.' I couldn't hear sound, not after they said that, and not now he sat down.

I continued like I was practicing sign language and he told us he was trans and he told me he would be happy for me to pass on his information to Safer Custody and I told him the LGBTQ group would be on this week and I would be there. Yes, I do go! Don't pull that blank face at me! I went a few months back!

We talked before they took me back, walked round the pool table so others didn't hear. Said he was nervous about being transferred here, said the other prison wasn't like this, he thought I was staff! All I could think was thank God I didn't wear sweatpants!, Did I put my mascara on? Like he would notice! Thank God I wore my best bra! Like he can see! But then he looked at me and smiled and I told him I was always down at the gym, maybe he might see me. I know I haven't been there in three months, I pulled a hamstring! Don't judge me, I have not changed. I hope that bitch Josie doesn't spot him, or Danelle - she split up with Lisa last week.

Goes to black. Jones stood knees bent head down hunched heavy breathing.

JONES: Ok, so change of plan, you're right. Canteen makeup is not a great idea for the gym. No, you're crazy, of course I didn't let him pair with me! I worked with Mandy, I can't let him see me heaving and sweating. Yes, I know I do, but that's different! I will be laying down! I need a shower!

Fade to black. Lights spotlight, JONES is sat reading, up in bed.

JONES: No, I don't want to talk about it, he's hanging around with that armed robber, Cal! We were sat in library, they came in and I looked over my glasses as they went to corner reading funny book titles, "Get Your Shit Together" and "My Shit Life" by Frankie Boyle. No, I haven't read it. No, I don't think they're funny!

Fade to black. Light comes up in an empty cell. JONES runs in and slaps the wall and spins round.

JONES: He is here! He's been moved to Lena's room - got her job as gym orderly too. Might have put his name forward... No, I didn't plan this! Lena was due to go back to Poland, she has been talking to me. I just waited to drop it in with Miss Jefferson, got off her annual leave. I'm not sly, I'm inside!

Goes to black. Spotlight appears on JONES facing the audience as if she's looking into a mirror putting lipstick on. Turning to the side, then the other side after she stops.

JONES: Prison mirrors always make you look like you entered a hall of mirrors - smudged and scratched. I guess I should be grateful plastic doesn't show how big my bum looks in this! Although I was on the stepper this morning and Martine and April were flirting. I said, "Why don't you ever say anything nice to me". He turned round and said, "Nice arse!" and walked off. Later we got told they're doing a film of Beauty and the Beast. I said, "well, when are you gonna take me out on a date?" No, I don't know if he did.

There's a knock. She walks to the side of the stage and smiles.

JONES: Hey you.

CURTAIN

Weather

Translated from Dutch from Ida Kerkhoff's 1978 poem from her poetry pamphlet 'Teken Van Leven'. A year before I was born. My mother.

As the words are
I pronounce myself
and I'm gonna be rain
and become
Sun and I become storm in rain

One hears me being
One speaks about me as
A result of not
Knowing anything anymore
That I am

And I become rain
Keep wind again

But not loved if I
Stay long

Poetry

My father's poem to my mother written with letters to Holland from England before I was born.

I thought poetry was drinking beer from beer cans
I thought poetry was eating fish in ink-stained paper
with greasy hands
I thought poetry was drinking vodka in half pint pots,
with a steady hand
I thought poetry was fighting bobbys on cold wet Sunday mornings
in London town.

I think poetry is a pretty Dutch girl
with a smiling face and shining eyes
I think poetry is a kiss in Venlo
A touch, a caress, a girl like you.

My Mother's Country

I don't remember the country
My mother was born in,
Only that she came here on holiday,
Met my dad,
I don't know how that was enough
To make her pack a world away
In a case?
Travel by boat, or was it by plane?
Far from her life of art, poetry and dance.
Library books and work.
Family and friends.
To start again.

I don't remember the pain she felt?
Or perhaps the excitement?

She told me once - every day is an adventure,
I have forgotten how I sat,
When she told me that,
When she went out and I went through her things,
I wanted to know her
The peacock as it called out to her
Like I imagine it did me
The smell of wet soil on Oma's allotment,
The dark places in Opa's garage
Where I would breathe in so hard my lungs would burst.
I think you would only know that?
The fish in the tank that stretched across a whole room.
The statues of Jesus and his wise men that spread out the Nativity.
The feel of cotton wool,
The silk patterns of woven blankets
Your mother made
But you could not.
Was it the same for you?
When I could not?
You never said once,
Maybe that was why you left?
In a language I new little of
But enough of.

They picked away at the threads.
But I remember your smile.
You never mentioned regret.

Each story you told me.
Each person you unfolded.
Like woven sheets
Was my bedtime story
My home is my country.
But my heart is here with you.

My Father

It was my father
Who first told me about Lot's wife
How women were cursed by their mistakes in the garden of Eden
Heed not my warning
He would often remark
Dark thoughts followed me
Shadows of hands crawling up my bed sheets.

My Seventh Birthday Party

The sports hall was only a walk away from our house,
No one could drive in my house.
We arrived early,
I felt so nervous,
Would they come?
Like thoughts of non-uniform day,
Walking, looking, waiting,
To see someone ,
to know you are not the only one,
Will I be the only one?
Am I the only one?
The trampoline loomed like the entrance to a secret passage,
On my neighbour's Sega,
That I got to play on,
Sometimes,
Sometimes I had to avoid his older brother,
Who stared at me and wanted to touch me.

I looked up as my mother pointed,
At bouncing bodies,
One at a time,
They were happy in their bodies,
I could not stand up,
I could not reveal myself,
For this body I had,
 was meant for someone else.

The Haunted House

Age 11

It was midnight in the haunted house
The doors were creaking wildly
and down below
the screaming noises of ghouls and ghosts
dancing through the night.

Mum Why?

Age 11

Mum do I have to go to bed now?
Mum why can't I read a book?
Mum why do you love Dad mum and why can't you get a job?
Mum why is John screaming mum?
Why has Dad lost his keys?
Mum I am getting tired now can I go to sleep?

In The Middle Of The Night

Age 12

In the middle of the night owls hoot
In the middle of the night birds don't sing
Soon it's morning,
Then I will be awake and the birds will sing once more.

Thunder And Lightning

Age 12

Thunder and lightning,
Comes once more,
It crashes and clangs
Like the bell on our door.
It comes at night
And ends at dawn,
The children are crying,
The cats are asleep,
The dogs are howling,
But me.
I am at peace
Once more.

Trees

Age 12

The shadow of the trees glisten in the night sky.
The fields shine in the moonlit evenings.
Moonbeams going in and out of houses.
I look into your eyes and I see the love.

Chimney Sweep

Age 12

Along the narrow alleyways
The ghost of the chimney sweep lies
His face as black as soot
But his eyes as dark as the night
He sits on every rooftop
Until the sun comes up
Then strangely he has disappeared
Until the night comes once more.

The Fair

Age 12

The fair is coming
Hurray, hurray and there we shall play!
The big wheel is tall and I'm very small
and that's the way I feel
but when I'm up high as big as the sky
I don't feel so small after all

Unmute

We are born to first words
Told to repeat until we understand
The words the people in our world want us to live by
We are simply repeating
Till it sinks in
Or it sinks us.

Born With Demons

I can't talk
Words distort
My body's rooted to the ground
Like tree trunks
I grow deep into the dirt
That's where you belong
I hear my head cry
Thoughts circling like moths to a flame
I can't be tamed
Tearing through fingernails finding nothing but filth
Buried alive
Time has cursed me
I paid the price for a life I hadn't lived yet
Tears before acts committed
My mind had ripped in half
Laughed and stood
Hooded in front was my heart
You are the enemy
The enemy within
Surrender.

Stories in the Dark

We are under the sheets
It keeps us warm
Our fort in a storm
My twitching eyes peek out once in a while
(children's limbs are not designed to stay still for long)

I wiggle out defiantly

Don't leave
a whimper deep inside echoes out to the surface
in hoarse bubbles like Morse code

The land below is lava
 the vast area of red is death
 to those who seek to tread

I lift a foot
almost feel the heat spit up like it burns

I go back into our covers
see shadows on the wall evaporate

Within this chasm between bliss unashamed
and thick landscapes made through laying still
I never noticed the other person leave.

Coercive Control

I try to be quick
so as not to let you notice
my hand is shaking while I cook
If you look up now you'll know

I drop the egg

'You stupid bitch.'

You know just where to punch
So all my scars are internal
Like my trauma as it turns my skin red with your slaps
I try to laugh and nod when you talk
But when you suddenly stand up
I jump

'You stupid bitch'

You surge forward
my eyes explode in tears
no impact
as you walk away laughing
I try not to
I try not too
I lock myself in the bathroom just so I can silently scream
I try not to
I try not too

Damnatio Memoriae

If I become what I fear then the fear disappears.
souvenirs from past abuse
Stuck to fridges
on postcards
Hung on my wall
In paintings
That line my mind
When I close my eyes
I look at the mirror Inside
I see that it's wrong
But when I open my eyes
It can't be undone.

Staying Human

What do I feel?
Bouncing on childhood trees
Watching in the branches
Laughing
How no one could see me
No one could ever see me

I was hidden like the trees
Held captive
In pine needles, smells, dreams.
So dark
Outside was the dream
No one really had seen
I yearned for peace

What do I feel?

Like that day in the trees
Before my deeds defined me
Before life made branches break
Under the weight of me.

Postcard A Day

I met her,
On the exact day
I had decided to give up,
It was only natural,
As I pondered life through too many pints,
As the glass was near empty,
I thought, *this is not what I want,*

I sat there,
Listening to the music,
Listening to the people
Like ants all in line,
Getting to the top of the mount,
I didn't know the rules,
But in that moment I chose,
To stop and there you were,
A hand so confident
'Do you want to dance?'
My feet never hit the ground,
The thought of leaving you,
Even after just meeting you,
Made me feel more than I ever had,
So promises were made,
My best pulling jumper left on your bed.
A postcard a day.
Till I returned to what I wanted:

Day was sunny, I miss you. Can I say that so soon? I walked to the
plane to miss the thought of not even being blessed to be in the same
country as your smile.

I awoke thinking of you
Is that too much?
Since we met I can't do much more.
We walked through woods,
Old familiar family journeys
With new thoughts,
I wanted you to see,
Where I come from?
I wish you were here.

Devolution

When did we go
from laying in the sheets
To lying to each other?

Each step
like a what's not to do guide for lovers

Undoing
I do

Unrevealing our flaws
That we peel back like our clothing
When love was all there was to talk about.
passing in the summer breeze

We used to chase
To a slow pace
Untalking
Unliking
Unthinking
Like walking backward through a door
Where can you start?
When were you started?
Got you here
Year after year
Till the face on the other side of the sheets
Turns from a smile
To a side profile
To a back
To a space mission
Black holes replace BlackBerrys
Technology has advanced
We no longer need to shout
Just relive the same three dots
That stop
Till we reach 1%

I Try Not To

I feel like deja vu
Like every drop of me there's you
Standing over me as I mop, hoover, wash up
I try not to stand up straight as you say
'I am using my height as a weapon against you'

I am not allowed to smoke outside
When others can whenever they want
I try not to roll my eyes
You say;
'I do it every time.'

I lock myself in the bathroom and try to breathe
My heart is heaving but I can't leave
I try not to look you dead in the eyes
'What are you starting up this time?'

I try to find myself at work but too many shifts
and I am having an affair
I try to budget with what you give back to me
But you tell me:
'My wages never cover anything.'

I look in the mirror and can't believe I am in between
I get thrown up against the wall with her hand around my neck
'But what did you do wrong to cause this mess?'

My mind's bent like branches
As they circle me
The apples are gone along with my sanity
It's a hat trick
As I face each hurdle I know it's the final chapter

Ogenblik

I leave the House only this time I know I'm not coming back
Memories stare blankly in the new flooring I had put down
The dogs already leaving pockmarks
My worn walk as I trail through
The cupboards with new handles for someone else to use
The window letting in the morning air tastes of an old life now
packed inside a suitcase
My case big enough to put me in a place away labeled like winter
coats for another day
I step out into the warm rays
As they hit my face
As I leave this place
My life is locked behind me.

Flash Bulb Moment

The stage is set
The lights go up
The spotlight bright
You can't give it up
The scripts In front
The life of filter
The life of us
One day the hero
Then the villain
The starting blocks
The method true
Online destruction
Is an Olympic sport
All rise to the crown court
Sharing online stories
With no remorse
Your imaginary part
Social media activist
Playing devil's advocate
Regardless of who's right.

It's A Lovely Day But I Am Dressed Like Winter

I sat there sweat dripping
Dipping out of consciousness
Court clothes once smart
Now pressed wet like chainmail against my chest
and in my mind I thought of all I had lost

I felt myself drowning in concrete boots,
sparks exploded
neurons fired out like empty barrelled shotguns

I saw myself at fifteen
no one there to tell me any different
of what one split decision could lead me to
paths that only lead here

No one no one
no chance of someone coming back in time
to tell me how to divert an apocalypse

Yet you replay the warning
like it would be the undoing
of everything you're feeling right now

Stop
One day you're going to have to answer to yourself
The price of this moment will continue its debt
way after it's been paid to courts barristers and prisons

Stop
One day all the people you swore had power over you
will either be dead or left
and you will carry what's left

Stop now and realize
sometimes you have to accept the truth
(what is your truth?)
To fight the habits that form inside your mind
o simply soothe yourself

Get into the habit of asking yourself why you do what you do
how you are what you are
think why you think
Just Stop before the concrete sets in

Back When

It is not always as it seems
Through tears of victims' eyes
Across broken systems of wigs and screens
Not seen voices for their protection
Yet in these reflections
Where was my protection?

Back when things could have changed
Back when tears were not a permanent stain
On my pillow case at night
No one highlighted my blight
Yet now as courts decide a fate
To take a life
It's right

We are all here to address a crime
To serve the public's best interest
Defend victims
Clean the soiled hands
That bare witness

Back when it mattered
Was years before
I was untouched
My soul embarking on a world of adventure
No dent in my soul
No heavy hand on my shoulder
Telling me how to blind my eyes
Rip my heart into
Flick off the switch
To wait in blackness and denial
Till it's time to put it right

You hurt me
I hurt
I hurt you
Who knew

If I had the strength to leave
Maybe I could have walked out the door
To clean air
Not rows of cells and a slit window.

Sentence Served

Shh,
Sinking stomachs
Stinging, stigma, stains,

Shh,
Stirring, stifling
Stand still!
Stewing, steady

Shh,
Stammer, stall,
Stalemate,
Sitting Staff squinting

Shh,
Spotlight
Spellbound spectacular
Spectators sport

Shh,
Sweaty speechless sadistic
Shamefaced scandal says sun.

Shh,
Scrutinized, sealed, seamless
Seized, secure, security
Slammed, shouting.

Shh,
Shrink, shrivel, shudder, scared.
Sacrifice.
Silence, solitude
Solution solved.

Judge's Last Word

How we live with the before and afters
Are how we convince ourselves with stories
Of why people deserve what they get and why
they should pay for what they done

It's nothing more than a witch hunter trail
The way people need reason for things
happening to them and what answers
Leave reason as to how to explain them
If bad things happen to bad people
This must be a taste of how bad I am

No one looks any further then a crime
Not behind a story or a human life

I am frozen
Caught in the heights
Of then and now
Before and after
Past and present
Frozen

In that second before fear
Before the moment tips the waiter and you come from waiting
 to seeing
to happening
I'm floating in the seconds before
Frozen as we stand at the door and it is neither locked or unlocked
 it is just simply a door.

I am the way

The sponge in the electric chair conducting conditioning death
but not dying myself
only each sensory gland remembers burnt in to its core
 The moment of each minute dying
becoming everything
Yet the last breath always carries on

 I am my own last breath

Lovers

I bite my lip
Forget what it is to feel the touch of another
Met with cuffs
No jokes but blank eyes
I try to hide myself
Bubbling bottomless bellies of acid erupt like Mount Vesuvius
Too late as I choke back violent explosions
Staring out of slit windows
Traveling to my death
It's May
But not 1536
Yet the crowds entered through doors
To catch a glimpse of my downfall
To go home after I was taken
Sure of how they had convicted
Under a law
That's forged in power
Success that's built on the ruins of empires
The law saw no wrong in destroying all that stood in its way
To this day, let it be framed
I may not travel to my beheading
But I will forever be reminded of this
For the crowd never forgets
While the heart longs for better days
I think of past lovers
All soft skin and cheshire grins
Or long legs and angel smiles
The open eyes and open hands
That lead from youth to a noose
Now I'm here
I am still human
Now proven
Forever more
Just a criminal

Sit There

You sit in a room
Mum's out with your brother
Your dad's at work
You sit all alone
Dissociating
wishing you knew how to make it
You're sick of being told
To be a thing you're not
Till you start to lose the plot

You sit in classrooms
You sit in detention
You sit on door steps
Waiting wanting wishing
You sigh looking into empty cupboards
You lie and pocket dinner money
You sit in parks smoking
You sit fitting In
You sit drinking
 when you realise you never did

You sit at the back
Back of the bus
Back of the class
Back of the changing room
Finding space between you and all you forgot
Forgot all of you between finding space
All you did
All you had
Like bags in a station waiting to depart

You sit in interviews
A college room
A council office
A police station
You sit in pubs
Drink too much
Sit outside takeout shops

THE BOY BEHIND THE WALL by Dalton Harrison

You sit silent
You sit shouting
You sit wondering how you made it
You sit in clubs
You dance
You leave for the night
For the night to leave you
You end up starting over
Till starting over ends you

You wake up to be sick
You sleep to stop
You look up in a cell
You sit in the dock
You sit in prison
You sit behind barbwire
You sit trying to remember
where it all went wrong

The Doors Shut

In the silence.
In the sound of a single heartbeat.
I am blind.
Divined by the past.
Last to know my journey's road pump lies ahead,
Before I hit it instead.
I am spotting the blood of what if.
The pressure inside my mind,
builds in my concussion.
All I have is destruction.
I am the wreckage,
Of my own self wrecking ball.
Too self important to see the ants
I have trodden on.
I picked the fork in the road,
Choose the devil's tongue.
Well I am done!
I am undone.
It's begun!
Too small a space to chase my self loathing,
 I can't outrun.
Well I am done!
I will find the bricks left in this mess
To rebuild myself.

The Republic

This is now
This is all I see
Between the bed and the door
The sink and the floor
This is my Republic
My Justice
Yet I fail to see the wisdom

I wonder between the voices that scream on the landings
To the boots and radio that echo back at me
Behind the constant hum of conversations
That rise and fall on a wave of debate
What would Socrates have said?
'In the interest of the strong. I am here?'

My kingdom is mapped, its borders defined
Like the chalk marks of a crime
From bedpost to bedpost
If Plato believed that the world is both visible and intelligible
Where does that leave me?
I am tortured
Left in a man-made cave
to view the shadows on the wall
is my only reality

Paused

Time was the noose around my neck
Too late to prove who I was even to myself
I was a war
Battles fought and won on enemy lines
My lines crossed
My paths lost
Chalked out like crime scenes
I am unseen
Just left on pause

Karma

I'm stressed
A little vexed
Perplexed inside a caged beast
Least these surroundings are founded
I've landed in barbwire
I'm tired
Will I ever find release
I'm crying, trying to change fate, is it too late?

The law of karma's happened
The process a little haphazard
I'm living in delusion
More confusion
To transcend my actions takes action
Like a seed growing
In spite of all my efforts it festers

Good or bad actions matter
For they leave a mark on the psyche
This sways me to attain a deeper insight into reality
There's a strip of light that always hits me
when I turn out the light at night
Too much light ignites my mind in lines reflected off the bars
Reality could be happier
If I could find my way out
These tracks scorch my mind as I recount all that has gone before

When All Is Lost

Pride's place in prison
Hide the colour
Ride out the pain in marks you leave behind
with your own fingernails
I am nothing but the click in my back
as I stretch my spine in line with my will
as the door slams shut before I turn

Jekyll and Hyde officers
Dried stinging eyes forced behind bars
Slide along floors as you get pushed from behind
Decide who you gonna be before it's written in the marks
Dug so deep in wooden desks
Railings and walls imprisoned in the words *no place for pride here*

Ghosts

The night is long
Where prison pillows meet the sides of cheeks
To wipe away the streaks of tears
That travel down faces like street maps

Where in the distance
between me and you
mark the sounds of a life, once lived?
now merely ghosts to those who know them

Little strangers locked in cells
Listening and dwelling in the past
That cast shadows
Open hatches
Walk through walls to mark the spot
They once stood
one by one
Rattling doors

The only sound of the future
rests solemnly in these echoes
Like footprints behind walls
Banging to get out
The slow train coming
Passes with passengers
Never sees what's inside
Where tattoos mark walls
as history leaves
with only the banging of the bars

All I Have

I have cracks in my bowl
Can't you pour in the gold?
Told me I am ready to enter society
Tied to labels I tried to fit

I have cracks in my bowl
Can't you pour in the gold?
Talking over me
Till my choices are gone
All along I tried to hang on

I have cracks in my bowl
Can't you pour in the gold?
Tell me my future is not blamed
On my past mistakes
Am I too late?

I have cracks in my bowl
Can't you pour in the gold?
Hold my dreams just high enough to see
Can't you let me be?
Oh anxiety!

You Never Know

They say when you die
You see a long black tunnel
A door at the end
Then a bright white light

They let me out that first morning
Just another transfer on a list
New prison
New rules
Another hierarchy to manoeuvre round
Another induction
Another cell
Fresh fag ash on the slats and someone elses smell
Start again
Start at the bottom as a snake replaces the ladder
I stand at my cell door
Look back and forth like stepping out into oncoming traffic
I walk down a long black corridor
I open a heavy door to a bright white light
"Is this inductions?." I hear myself call out

There you are
Like life's moments expected you there
A smile so rare
Eyes like stars that formed
on all the lonely nights I made wishes on
My heart had already answered
When you replied
"Yes."

The Keepers

I will sentence you to time
befitting the crime

In this power
In this instant
I hear nothing
Just slow moving arms, eyes of dust
Sparks that ignite like gunshot
I smell burning
The flash like camera bulbs
Heat, so much heat

Maybe the gleaming corridors daze me into confusion
A delusion as I stagger alone
As locks click bracelets binding down arms
Wrists burn, faces flush
But in this stunned silence, no tears
Just the grip of fear
Rolling back inside

A fire bursts up out of my gut, raising, engulfing all
Like a back draft laying in wait
Yet no one opens the door

The screams are swelling
The need surges forward
It's just an action not designed to have a reaction
To anyone who witnessed my downfall
Society has locked that door
I belong no more
The chain reaction, the cylinder, the ammo explodes inward
I will sentence you to time,
befitting the crime,
in line with the law
Eyes hitting the floor.

The first sound of screaming, like a child being born
Many hands to expand this life into a world it doesn't know
A mystery

A sharp crack illuminated in thunder
Then simply white noise
A world of talking heads
That make no sense
Rows of blurred faces
Till one stands out
The one who sounds familiar
Yet you never understand
Why?

Yet in time
You face life, like a stream of blinking colours
in the tunnels of your mind
You shout out into a well, down into the echoes of darkness
See change as a door you would gladly keep shut
Feel only nothingness, smells like burning,
sounds like ripping nails on backboards
Nipping, squeaking rats forge a home
in the nests grown around nerve endings
Like balls of smoking flames, electrical fires of the brain
Behind doors of the soul
Uncontrolled

Fear the back draft
As it swells and moves behind ribs and lungs
Time become the crime
You give up
Till one day
Becomes two
As cruel as it sounds
Walls fences, barbwire
Shuts out more than societies hypocritical teachings
Get in line, form a queue, stack people
Body bags containing, one heart, two lungs
All in rows, wings, neat lines, attached to blood vessels
All joining up, no sound
But the clanking of locks into bolts into steel
Hard cold, stiff controlled, meticulous
Contain, detain, maintain
Reform lives
Anarchy

THE BOY BEHIND THE WALL by Dalton Harrison

Dehumanize
Deliberately define lives by crimes
Watch us all follow in line
Yet in this chasm
Deep within the screams
The calamity, the cataclysm

One voice speaks out,
Familiar
Although I know we have never met
It pierces through pockets of nausea
Slowly, nascent, stirring
Past the locks of old
Into where only isolation breathes
Where the corners of the souls blow in the wind
like tattered flags off broken sunken ships
Thrashing tides wash to and fro
Desolate, remote lands
The Gaol of the mind
In time no sentence can rupture it
Yet this voice erodes all
Unlocking the fireball,
the backdraft of pain explodes out into the world
This once insurmountable fire
Just burns enough to keep warm
This moment, this single light bulb, switched on
To see one person
Not millions of voices screaming out in pain
Then nothing but shadows faint steps
The keepers come
Nota bene
A quantum leap from legislative lemmings
But an iridescent quest at my rebirth
Whose guidance to the guilty
Opens more than just doors.

What Burns And Scars

You used to push your finger
In the top folds of the flesh
That rested on my arm
Something you said
Would remind me of you
When I looked down and saw finger marks
Maybe the time we spent away
Made it ok
As you were there and my fear of being alone had framed DNA
Yet in these marks
Like past abuse too frightened to lose
This mark felt safe.

Like all that was before was somehow easy
As I knew my way
Through the forks of fear
Paths of pain
Like chains weighing down cases
As I travel to find my place.

Before you
My love had left a bracelet of fingertips
so heavy in gold around my neck
The past echoed in the sobs of youth's bloodstained mattress
Leave only dancing scars
Like bangles in the breeze
As the moment forms faces and freezes
They only left the memory in places no one could detect
Healing under me now is a thought
That you are not right for me.

As I look into the past like a mirror shattered by denial
I enter a trail where I am the one
Who marks
Yet now
My marks burn reminding me
That there time was never spun in courts with wooden floors
Now the doors slam shut.

My fear of being alone has brought me in handcuffs
Scuffed floors
Record report restore
Order here
No more tears
The door slams shut
Only I never knew such a feeling
Nothing but me believing
No one's going to leave me jewellery tonight.

Asylum

Welcome to bedlam
I am laying here like I am delaying the inevitable
If memory foam mattress could talk
To prison mattress would they listen?
My mind's going mad but my heart won't listen
When did the asylum become the prisons?
What's the difference between workhouses?
So much neglect no one seems to detect
Where its populations rise rapid ridged rules from a Victorian era
Yet no one highlights the abuse
A fate sealed in ghosts walking into eternity
Were hands are still bound,
blood letting is left to those dubbed degenerates behind cell doors
in acts of despair
We wonder in the sins of generations that never repaired
Steel doors, morning calls, gloomy floors
Tripping with the sweat left by the dead
The past repeating like a stutter
Neglect and misery are door knockers
History has yet to receive its verdict
When time repeats society leaves
This is the new asylum
this is the next century.

The Overnight Wing

Shouting self-harming
Focus on the future now
Something to drive for.

Prison life

Despair some may say
It may be trivial to you
Hopelessness lives here.

The Catcher In The Rye

All I wanted was a book
The night was too long without the folds of paper to comfort me
My dreams relaid my fate
While walls and doors echoed the sounds
As I kept running unable to get out

All I wanted was a book
As I searched but only found cells and pin boards
I sat lost in memory,
Morning only brought a mouthful of mourning
A moment of half yawning
Then the dawning as you woke in a prison bed

All I wanted was a book
Like an addict I looked
With the desperate need that made my heart fear
That if the day ended without this one thing
Maybe tomorrow wouldn't come for me

All I wanted was a book
Each line of the spine
like somehow knowing I have this
would make me whole again
I am a shadow
Unseen and therefore somehow unreal

All I wanted is a book
Like when my mother took me to where she used to work
Like when those who knew her before me
Said she was their boss
The head librarian
Before books went into computers
My mother was the one to go to
The one who memorized every line
That had it all alphabetised
All I wanted was a book

All I wanted was a book
Like the times in summer holidays
When all you have is sat on shelves
Each an adventure, a friend,
The only thing that keeps you sane
That one book that changed everything
That narrative that represented something you couldn't breathe
To anyone,
Yet here it is.

"Sir, please can I pick a book off this shelf?"
'Only one. Make it quick'
The Catcher in the Rye

You

What do you do
When life is not a phone click away?
Not a Facebook fix
Snapchat filter
Instagram story

What do you do when
You go from believing people care
Because they share or like your posts
To sharing the news that features your story?
You become nothing but voiceless
Clickbait to someone else's narrative

What do you do
When you go from being live
To being here?
Four walls
Just people walking and talking
Instead of looking into screens
that show them all the ways to connect
except to the reality we're in

What do you do?
When all you knew about the world is handed in
Bagged up and sealed
Batteries taken out
When it goes from what you have
To what you can carry
To what you're allowed in

What do you do
When all there is, is you?

The New Normal

First few days go by in a daze
Dining hall hits you with a perfume of gloom
Then boom plastic tray flying through the room
Like a newsroom hits breaking news
teams of black and white rush in
Pull apart fists, hair and plastic knives
I want to get out of this mess but the test is there's nowhere to hide

One week in the dining hall
Still feeling the doom as my eyes check the room
I am hazy and shaky as I long to get the food
A girl runs out the room,
tries to throw herself off the top fire escape
The crowd's shouting
Some people hope she does it
As she goes head first, an officer grabs her legs
My head's bouncing
but now the shock's not got me counting heart beats like it once was

Who can say in a year
Looking round like I have always been here
Eyes don't need to look as deep
Seen suicides, fights and tears
Can feel the tension before it breaks out in blood
Screaming snapped knives and eyes streaming red
Officer's not ready and it goes on too long
I cover my meatloaf and watch the show

One Week

I ask you this:
Do you listen to the lies you tell yourself,
Hate fuelled using insanity as a tool
you sentence yourself over and over again
To live a life of walls and barbwire
Where if anything comes close it gets ripped up and torn in half?

I ask you this:
What going make you reassess
This mess
This so-called life of hate and regret
This abyss, this loop of old home moves of drugs abuse and booze?

I ask you this morning:
Did you bind your hands
to stop from clawing your eyes out at the reality
That all this hate and pain never got you nowhere?

I ask you this when we stand in line for medication
Wait to be called for association
Line after line
Time after time
Just two steps to anywhere:
Is this all there is?

The Boy Behind The Wall

Walls pot marked from pillar to post
Marks left like the pictures of the first moon landing
Holes left behind like relics
Absent drawing pins define walls and corridors like gunfire
What's left is bound together by masking tape and rubble
Buckled by the weight of bodies rotting
Exhibits of a cultures lack of humanity
Lock em up, ship em out
Nothing but limitless time, bouncing in space
The space inside the crater that society built
I had landed in another galaxy
Behind the wall of dark matter
Nothing mattered
There was no gravity
No one to hear me scream
What identity?
What are you here with me?
A number
A letter
A place among floating debris
Space junk falling slowly back to earth
What are you here?
No air
Just hula hoops of time
Round and round
I'm just a satellite signal to far
I am just the boy behind the wall
Trying to make my mark

Chained

This is England
Through the prism of journalism
Wisdom of a point system
Over who can get the most likes
You never look at the individual
Only the police state
That leads to the courts
then the prisons and the probation system.
This is great Britain
a tradition twisted in Executions
Our kingdom is built on prisons
Who house more victims
Than are listed
Their names existed
But there past never scrubbed out
no last meal
Last deal
Their heels didn't even drag on the ground
False fed food forgotten in rooms
Framed displayed in an exhibit
Art becomes life in one take
In all that pain
 no one listened
Take me home
Only there is no such place
Memories that no longer
have brick or a face
Like they no longer have a base
Hate walks in-between alarms
Fairytales of life on the outside
Dismissed like gates to freedom's cries
Yes we walk in the moments we made
Yes we talk in the hell we can't tame
But where in the humanity is there to lay my head
In this justice system
is only the hostages of vengeance
chained.

At Night

I grab the bed sheets
Like I would an old coat
I walk down the dark streets
Of where I used to live
Lights shine in windows lit
Street lamps twinkle like stars
I remember nights like these like old lovers keeping me warm
I walk to the beach
Hear the waves crashing
Like all the days that broke
On white hot foam
Between then and now
I embrace the night
The sounds
The strength and weakness of being alone
But I never was
I am here
Following myself
Walking in the night
Closing my eyes
Longing for sleep
Searching for a home

Just Me

I was never meant to be perfect
Hurting lonely controlled forgotten
I was never meant to be me
Born to parts that made me want to rip and cut out my existence
like a jigsaw piece
I was never going to be validated
I didn't love myself all I was lay waiting in the dark of me
Teasing tortured tones
Prison was already built in me
A prison inside a prison
So what was reality?
I was never meant to be perfect
Learned nothing to teach me otherwise
Time crime punishment
I would cry but I haven't stopped since I was a child
I was never meant to be me
The cord cut I was tangling free
But heavy was the load
I landed behind locked doors
 I was never meant to be perfect
Hurting lonely controlled forgotten
Till I saw the image after weeks of no mirrors
I saw the truth
I saw myself
I saw beneath the broken skin
I was never meant to be anything
Now it's my time to be my everything

I Am

To the world
I am here

To the Governor
I am on a transfer list

To the officers
I am a number, a cell, a room
A standfast roll check

To the courts
I am filed in offices

To the media
I am a crazy-eyed picture

To society
I am a Google away

To the streets
I am the lining in old newspapers
To someone's bed

To the wind
I am a whisper through bars and gates

To the sky
I am just a pair of eyes
Looking up at it all
To the clouds
A little smile at funny fluffy patterns

To my family
An empty place at the dinner table

To myself
But a shadow slowly taking shape
Without a trace of what I used to be
Between dark matter and space.

My Face

Do you hate this face
Laced with lines of taint
Fate has parted our ways to late
Created in my blue eyes
Echo evidence I left behind
Lies told to hold
Onto nothing
Lucky you
May chuckle
Thinking I am gone

Do you longer long
On the child's eyes left behind
To see the blue ocean drops
My tears left in his eyes
In our one last goodbye.

The Question

Have you ever cut yourself?
Consumed you stare
Frozen, wide eyed and rooted,
You want to lose it,
Call out for help but you're too focused
The skin surrounding the surface
The colour so bright,
yet dark…

Have you ever broken bones?
The pain,
the body sweating, swelling round the muscle,
the mind, distracted, contracting in spasms,
as the part becomes alien detached unworking
not a part of the whole,
but now a burden…

Have you ever burned yourself?
feeling the sensation before the weld and emotions,
before the scare to warn you from future notions,
that lead to explosions,
of damage of DNA,
of trauma like a map to never again…

Have you ever dropped a cup,
watched as it fell marked only by gravity,
or your unbelieving ability to accept cause and effect?

Have you ever sent a text
or posted a message or sealed an envelope,
unable to unattach, unsubscribe, un-finish
that final decision to make it real?

Have you ever seen a family member die,
their eyes glaze,
no longer a person you knew,
they move out of the vessel they rested in and you're left all alone?

Then you will understand the wide-eyed
tilt your head to the side
question;
'what's it like going into prison?'

Then you will know the answer to the question,
you're really asking,
inside the exact moment
of how you would feel
when the cell doors click shut
for the very first time.

Love

Maybe I didn't recognize love for what it was
Maybe it didn't recognize me
What I had before wasn't what love stood for
So why would it know I needed it
Maybe I didn't recognize you for what you were
But somehow I did when I sat next to you
I knew I felt something

Maybe I didn't recognize me
That when I am with you
The world is connected
No longer a mismatch, a patch-up job of regret

Maybe when I knew
somewhere deep inside of me
Deep inside of here
That as each door locked,
I found other ways to see

Maybe I knew when I was still hanging on
to the past like a shard of glass
That if I stopped the pain
Reframed and changed
Love like a winged butterfly wasn't so scary
That with each beat of its wings
Love turned into a volcano
Red, orange, yellow, gold and silver

Maybe when I looked at you like you looked at me
Felt our first kiss
We both knew love wasn't going anywhere

Constricted View

Since the verdict was called
When I tried to stand tall
I turned and held out my wrist
Like wearing handcuffs was just a bracelet
Led through my first door
As it shut behind
I had a constricted view as fear turned me blind
Now softly lit lights play hopscotch on my cell wall
skies of blue call to me like an old friend
Rain hits my face if I slide myself through the bars
It's just a constricted view

If I lay in my bed
Look up and tilt my head
I see rolling clouds
See the earth move
See birds fly
It's just a constricted view

So I wait in that space between my window frame
Where I have no sense of time
Lines on walls shift in shadows
I see pigeons, buttercups, daisies swaying against the breeze
I have yet to feel
But oh,
When I tilt my head
It's just a constricted view

Let my heart learn to heal itself
Sore up over lush green treetops and fly again
Till I can find all my dreams and make them whole
To find me inside its folds

Resilience

I pace the cell
Almost delirious
I know I will get out
Bullying voices echo in my mind
I will have to face them
One by one
Oblivion plays tricks as it grips my insides
There is no reason I can find
To let my demons out to fight
I made a promise
In all the silence of that wagon ride here
With all those internal screams
That stripped me naked as I showered in reception
I will never fight again just because I'm scared
I will never let my life be taken from me

Time

What is this time
If full of care
We have no time to stand and stare

As I dare to stare
I repeat these lines inside my mind

A shout, heads turning, food falling
a girl being carried off

I detach myself
becoming inward eyes
designed only to stand and stare

The hallow ring to each step
on long shiny lands
the hum of voices like electric wires
sparking in the dark

everyone pretending there something there not
those who scream remain echos in the din
a voice cut thick
someone stole her washing
her family were in another time zone
she could never ring when they were in.

days on the landing feel like weeks on paper
she hanging she hanging

Dull black boots shut us all in

Once Upon A Time

My once upon a time
Happened years ago
I was all cheeky grins
A mop of blonde hair
I would listen to my mother
Tell tales of magic
Building the very fabric of my youth
My mother waving dreams
Her soft voice soothing me to sleep
Deep forests, logs burning, candlelight
Thoughts of fairies, pixies, angels in flight

My once upon a time
When magic fell down like snowflakes
On adventures where I was always the hero

A million books away now
From the start of my once upon a time
But the love remains
Every time I say my mother's name
Where the magic still echoes deep inside

Identity

What is identity inside these walls,
Doors so thick it binds the chest you hide so you can't breathe,
Define me by numbers,
a sign that says female estate,
I can't deny I'm here,
but I'm just visiting,
Yet still I see the dirt tracks of ghosts walking in rows,
the smell of death
like somehow that was the only way to ever be free,
What is identity,
identify me in societies hollow walls,
where no one hears you cry in towels,
given used and repeated
in a system that deals with mass incarceration,
this blue towel in my hand that I leave the streaks in,
my sobs, my grief, my guilt, my past,
I could wring it out, tear it in half in anger,
But I sit with this feeling that stretches across from hand to hand
I look and wonder in the middle of my pain
in the pinnacle of my fallen tears,
if anyone used this as a noose to stop theirs,
I throw it aside and it coils around like a viper in the room,
I feel the poison, I taste it on my lips,
I feel it in my body,
what is identity,
the system is they/them,
I am the boy behind the wall and the sign says female estate.

Who Are You?

Are you the pictures on the wall?
The wardrobe that could fill a room?
Car keys attached to places you been on chains and colours?
Are you a set of house keys that's duplicated for your family?
Are you all your dreams
In old record collections
Books and cuddle toys won at fairs?
Are you all your hopes in magazines
of best life to lead and what to eat?
Are you pots and pans?
Chairs that sink into the shape of you and one more?
Are you the television white hot static of movies
subtitled by laughing?
Are you sticky fingers and snacks?
Group chats and phones all out?
Are you selfies and hot drinks on lazy weekends?
Are you bliss in woolly jumpers?
Are you joy in padded jackets and fur trimmed hoods?
Are you complete in big towels and steaming showers?

Who are you?
A headline of the worst day?
Your biggest mistake?
Too late, too late?

Who are you?
A tearstained image caught in dry mouth, no filter haze?

Who are you?
No answers, book in your valuables

Who are you?
A file, a lock a bar some cuffs

Who are you?
The best and worst of society
Everything you thought you was but look what it cost
All you know is you're none of the above

Association Time

When you live in isolation
When everyone's on medication
Where the only release is education from incarceration
Information gives you keys
Communication is the only vacation you're ever going to see
A revelation to what could have been
Walk around yards like caged beasts
Being watched in the prison version of Big Brother
Telling stories but there's no campfire
I used to be a teacher
I used to be a door supervisor
I used to work as a care worker
I used to drive a car
I used to be in the C.I.A,
Wait, not sure about that one

Where bells sound with the misappropriation of power
No explanation is required
All that you own is subject to volumetric control
But when I look at the sky
Imagination has no limitation and the only way to keep me from
victimization inside these walls
I fight institutionalization watching clouds making shapes
while wondering what those in planes can see of our world
Sitting out in association
Walk and talk and greet in a box yard that's got only concrete
(even animals in zoos get grass)
Walk around in circles there is no straight lines
Look over fences, look over barbwire,
Past flood lights, past brick
To civilization
Where I will find salvation is all the motivation I seek

Prison Addict

I see walls to tall
Talking heads turn
You learn to watch and wait
Late behind dark eyes
 in dinner queues you see them pass
Last out they carry addiction
To addicts not yet ready to leave the green mile
Tired they lock themselves in before it's time
Line after line

Break
breathe in, in
savour it
Falling facing fabric fantasy final

Break
breathe out, out

Says Venus to the fly *come sit with me for a while*
Repeat the line as you trade behind bars
the dealer taking more than they ever could outside

Hungry

I am hungry
It breeds in me
As if the lives inside these walls are just here to cross pollinate
What's sinking into me spreads across me like war

I am so hungry
Tortured and desperate
I toss my head back trapped in this room
as if gulping in air will save me

I am hungry
Longing looks outside of windows
Glazed eyes stare into eternity
That echo each bar stripped face that press against them
Letting daydreams rip and tear at the fabric of reality
In my mind no time can touch me
yet it's killing me now

I'm hungry
Mind racing as if I am running on all fours

I'm hungry
When will they unlock my door?

BeLIEve

Read the poem as 'believe' or as 'LIE'

I beLIEve
I try not to beLIEve, I'm evil
beLIEving is all I have
It's all I have ever known
But here I am
beLIEving even after all I've seen and been through
like it's nothing
Yes,
I still beLIEve
But as the clock ticks to midnight
All my beLIEf does is eat away at my soul
What remains, I ask myself
What am I?
Do I beLIEve to save me
Or let guilt tame me
In pain I suffer to a future I can be proud of
Do I beLIEve in everything, you ask
I beLIEve in love
I beLIEve
I beLIEve
Because I can
My head in my hands
Looking through metal bars
I need to stop beLIEving and just change

StandFast

The hours pass
They last too long
The shadows dance
Like fireside companions
Only it's cold
I'm told it won't always feel like this
These fits of despair
My heart beating like bullets against my rib cage
Dazed into staring
Daring to move is too much
as my thoughts taunt me
Looting memories and setting fire to the dry leaves
 that fall all around me
The wind traps me inside
This wind trap this is all I feel now
How do I make it?
Take it while dreams
stab me
hatch out of me
I cry out
I found my way to morning
Unlocked
then a StandFast

Paused

Time was the noose around my neck
Too late to prove who I was even to myself
I was a war
Battles fought and won on enemy lines
My lines crossed
My paths lost
Chalked out like crime scenes
I am unseen
Just left on pause

Within These Walls

My mind summons demons
On rocks edged by time
I glide bare foot on barren landmarks appear gradually
increase only when I stay in place for too long
as I try to balance it cuts me deep
I travel on different plains of emotional strains
I wonder in labyrinths
Opening door after door
I bind wounds to hide life's mystery
I was born to shuffle blindingly along my body's man made curves
Yet not be made a man by them
Once I layed down and sunk so deep when I stood to leave the valley
filled with my own tears
I am a vagrant in society's trusting hand
let go when I didn't look like I could manage to walk the line
Tombs like Pharaoh's chambers
Mark my history as well as my grave
I dig deep beside strangers
not knowing as much as them
what will uncover
day after day
I am a searching through inward eyes at myself
unable to reattach my voice
an echo that travels further than I'm able to run

A to B

The corridor
Yeah that's the place to meet
Thunder on the landings
Rubber soles squeaking
Music blasting
New girls stuttering
Tough girls shoving
Culture in our corridors
A wonder of colours, conversations and accents
When all you have is you
Four walls and bars
The corridor is a festival of arts
It provides you with all you need and more
Dinner, doctor, dealer, sir, Miss or officer
In the corridor you find all the people that hide away in offices
Nothing sweeter than shouting
"Hey you said you were going to sort out that thing for me!"
The corridors too long to run
they end up staring like some curator at a spot above your head and
nod squirming like a worm
Till you laugh and walk off

In The Public's Best Interest

I am struggling almost tunnelling creating bunkers in my mind
Hideaways to hoard my failures deep within
I am a crime
A time to serve

Underfunded therapy
Waiting lists
A box of misplaced symptoms
We have no history here
Only rejected as mysteries
No identities just deficiencies
Down with crime
Up the times

We seek answers in checklists
Textbooks and most recent treatments
Used on who?
Pushback therapy
Increase drug dependency
Dissolve patient's file under criminal
Ex offender,
Risk profiles and crisis plans
what havens are left to aid dependents of the system
Re house there is none
how do I make it out of prison?
How do I survive inside?
A witness to inhumane visions
Down with crimes
Up the times
Is this 1984
Are algorithms the new thought police?
We only see what we want
But does that make it right?

Living

I'm living in the past
Swimming in a bowl of glass
I smash my way out
But only hit the surface
I gasp, breathe in air
Sink back down to try again
I'm living in the past
Memories fade but feelings last

Season's Greetings

Anxiety is a variety box of chocolates at Christmas,
It appears smaller, more expensive
Less of your favourites,
You find the attachment to what you imagined the way it used to be,
all consuming,
Like Scrooge you are visited by ghosts,
shouting unmercifully,
You are driven by fear,
it's clear you are all alone but the image is imprinted,
you see the echo in each meeting,
You lock the door but you turn to see them grinning,
like a reflection you twist away hoping that it will change,
The light goes off and on,
Eyes appear behind the door through smeared plastic,
Like a silent movie with no subtitles,
Your eyes feel like someone lit a match next to your face,
puffy red changing facial features,
You see only flash cameras,
You see people shouting,
You see dark,
You see the light touch the barbwire,
You see rainbows in dawn's outstretching arms,
That carry you out past these walls, past the doors,
Taking you to heaven,
its breath escapes like it's been waiting,
My last day, my last vision, Light!
Gate keepers calling me back to the shouts,

I resist, don't take me from this bliss,
Falling down, I feel hands,
My breath is back,
I can't hold out,
The light is gone,
I'm back in my cell,
The locks, the bolts, the lines of graffiti, the walls, the bars,
The officers radio blurred through waves of gasping and moaning,
Cold blue code blue
A wing, a room, a moment to soon,
to think of anxiety and selection boxes,
how I need those ghosts to stop,
no music loud enough,
I can't turn it off..
I can't turn it off..

The Officer's Dilemma

In time you learn
Turn the clocks back, it's not changed much
Seen that one through her teenage years
That one covered herself in her own shit chasing the dragon in here
Dignity not known by those who smuggle drugs
Inside their minds is black
You can see it in their eyes
Mug shot mugged off just slam doors shut

I can't see past
The visit halls so many children
Smearing sweaty fingerprints on windows
separating them from any chance of a childhood
That girl who screamed last night
I flicked her light on
She pissed the bed
Said it was her hot drink she spilt
We both knew the flasks don't keep much hot after one o clock
I asked if she needed a listener
She laughed it's alright
It will have to be

Tears fears these girls have em all
But keep ya guard up
seen them take officers down
With Mountains of debt on the wings
so they can get ghosted out
Crocodile skin and fake grins
They bite
 they bite
You can be sure of that

Fact is I know they could have been
My mother, my sister, my cousin…
what separates a journey?
Born into pain, a bad day,
a wrong turn, who can say?
All I know is
I will be that officer who notices

The Silence In Your Mouth

The staff are like fish they always forget
You're only good as what you're doing next

One step out the office
Swept out like the dirt
What you do on the landing
Should be seen but not heard
Lost to their tea breaks
They don't hear a word
Slammed doors in your face
They cuff your words

Everybody here is human
But no one's looking through doors
No one hears the sound
Of the screams behind the walls

The Good Officer

In dreams we perceive
All we hope to be
Diving in pools of rich colour
Changing to what only we see
Few wake to embrace such realities
For the dreamer
It will always be just a dream
Few believe after waking
All these colours can be achieved
But inside these walls and these stone floors
I found you believed in me

The Horror Story

Long winding corridors
Banging,
Keys rattling
Footsteps shaking the floor
Then stop
A bang of a shutter
Eyes melt from darkness
Grips the heart of a marked man
Pockets of air, raise curtains
A whisper? A shout?
I hear the tick of a clock
Then stop
It was midnight before I picked up the book
Run my fingers over the spine
Like my spine shifting against the plastic of my own bed
Slipping my head under
A breeze whirled from under door like the smoke of hell
I turn the page one by one
As if counting my own years
an alarm sounds
Then stops
Creaking chains around belts stalk the floors
beyond my chamber door
I read on
Hearing a scream gurgle deep within the folds of sleep
The book falls to the floor
A horror story

Surrounded

Prisons number one diet is the
sycophants diet,
Monday's start by working up to a slow burn workout,
Pick a fight with a sycophant
Burn five hundred calories,
Tuesday's don't go into the kitchen before twelve,
Were calling it the sycophants dance while fasting,
Wednesday avoid sycophants
Don't eat in the kitchen,
Lose a stone.
Thursday home in on your skills at ripping open packages of food
to show your disdain at them,
therefore ensuring the contents may be uneatable.
Deduce that from final calorie count.
Fridays Complete the duck and dive pre workout vibe,
to the toilet or shower to avoid all sycophants you may encounter.
Saturday session includes
hundred calories burn,
while ranting to yourself.
Try High impact pacing
in-between listening to them talking together,
a further fifty with added squats.
Practical when they peer through your hatch – you're not in!
While Sundays shadow boxing to them singing their hymns of praise
to the officers one hundred and fifty with a jog bounce of rage
another hundred
concludes your
sycophants weekly diet plan.

To All The Forgotten

You preach to me
Like fathers before you
You seek puppets on strings to please you
Now my strings are cut
Loose joints and forgot
Replace pictures on mantel pieces
Clear out clothes like winter is over
When love has taken wings and flown
The last feathers of decay wither in its nest
I am alone with your voice
Telling me I am poison
Changing the story as if you had the power to write it all along
You told me for years I played a victim well
Now you tell those who are left you were that victim
While writing this letter
You blame me
Like your mother blamed your father
I wonder how history finds its way to repeat

Storage Vaults Of The Mind

I sit in my cell
Detained, ashamed
No longer able to speak out
Four walls, a corridor, a wing full of echoes
Shadows, faces, walls
A forgotten society
Left waiting for roll call

All around fragments
Encased in broken hearts
Final screams of goodbye
Babies ripped away
Families on their knees
Begging pleas to no appeals
To dream
In nights almost silent creeps

Each cell, each room
Illuminated cubes
A beating heart
A hope, a need
To find your voice again
To speak out
Forgive me.

Visit Day

I trace my fingers
Across dirty walls
Graffitied and worn
Torn fabrics like a tapestry of a life in turmoil
Inside I find only lost souls
Controlled by
Told by
A system where you count the days
Till I can gaze into a rush of racing stars
An explosion of infinite space between us
Imploding into one

The Visiting Room

A rumble, voices loom
Faces peek like children against windows at a zoo
The outside stares back
Picking out familiar figures
Wondering, forming opinions, guess work or face
Silence descends
Matching faces from one side of the room to the other
Like a game of guess who
Still separated by a clipboard
Statues in black and white come alive

You!
Me?
Table six!

I step into the divide
Embrace the smell of love
Soft, hot
That's enough!
Sit down!

Beaming faces
Talking, a volcano of words, streaming, filling the room
Don't hold hands!

Eyes, lips, cleavage
I miss you
I love you
That's it, everyone say goodbye!

Too soon
One last look
Stand up!
Take your shoes off, mouth open, step in line, get your cards!
Silence!

Faces get hit by the cold
Bars shutting as they slice the air
Back inside, the room lets out a sigh

One O'Clock

Gunshot fires inside my mind
At night
I look through old books of my life
But still can't cry
Time ticks silent in a second hand clock as the battery died
The owner in-between life
I wish I could sit with her tonight
Whispering winds pass through the gap in the door
I lay in the dark
I wonder when night will end
Before sleep?
Or after the sun checks in
I can't hear for the sound
Of all I never said
I can't breathe after I left
Maybe it's the trees
So many leaves
Falling to the floor
Building bridges back to you
Or is this time the only time
arguments should not be left just before bed

Finding Hope

Time to hope
In all the time I have I find scope
In this hope that washes over me like soap
I know the days will be half broke if I look at my cup as half full
Compose myself after each nightmare
and approach each day with a little more care
Expose myself each time to the idea hope can be there
Then maybe I can learn to cope in the days my horoscope makes me
want to tie a rope to my bars, so I can choke
That hope is still there if only I make time
to turn the telescope the other way round
 unfold that envelope
To find a letter from my mother
and know that's all the hope I need right now.

Overqualified

When I was 19
I went into the jobcentre
Sat at her desk
Told her as she looked at my file
I wanted to be a prison officer
She laughed
Said I did not have the skills
Who's laughing now?
I have been here nearly two years

A part of me

A part of me
Has fallen
Crestfallen
Calling out but no one's there

I watch the secrets
I watch the scene

I saw myself fall
Bawling only to self-pity and regret

A part of me
Has risen
I see myself
Reflective in the gutter's waters
As my head hits concrete

A part of me
Has fallen
But a part of me has already got up

I slip between
Like memories scattered throughout time
Lies designed to keep you
Lies designed to keep me

Yet still we rise

Growing Wrong

First published in anthology 'Bloody Amazing' 2020

They never gave me the words
For fear of teaching me
How to be all the nightmares a parent doesn't want their child to be
I was born only to find as I grew
my body betrayed me
becoming a cancer
growing parts that were surely not meant for me
Met with suspicious eyes over dinner
night after night
I hid new words acquired by black market trading
Longing to learn the language to aid me
But my body bleeds oceans of red
Month after month
I can not part myself from its hex
I can not change the rage I feel
Deal with the smug look of this is the way that things should be
What is this slow agonising death
To spot blood and pay for aids to conceal and contain
To hate myself for giving me away
Guilt, shame,
Pay then display
My words are mimed
I am male
I am male
My words are both found and lost in a society that says
you are born this way
your paperwork says

Leave The Third Exit On Route

I was born to a roomful of cheers
Christmas morning dawning
Crawling out into the world
Hurled into the light

The first mistake set in steel
A bouncing baby girl they said
Met society in white lace
and wheeled in a cream wagon for all to see me
Feel nothing but splinters
A trojan horse sent to troy
Just a toy, I smile for approval

The second mistake forged in ironcast
The iron age begins
With a golden fleece of mopped hair
A mane of rich curls
Like corn in sunrise
Reaching little hands up to claim my mother's breast
I wait to grow

In all this perfection
Rejection breeds in me like leeches sickly feeding
Unaware how many have latched on
Along the route of which way is youth
I forgot to take in the view
Look around till I found a piece of me
I could count on
Along the path to adulthood
Blurring, turning back was not an option
Lost in chunks of armour, now impacted
I spent twenty two years
Putting in a flag
In societies check points of fears
Hear me
Look at me
But I was just another boy
Who put my finger in a dyke
To stop the water coming out

THE BOY BEHIND THE WALL by Dalton Harrison

I kept on walking, never stopped to long in one place
In case I was found out
Chasing the future in dreams of the past
Black mist and charcoal
Shaded in murials of what I had left in pride
Hide, hide, a lie defined

My third mistake
Am I late?
What's the time?
Lining up in queues
Lose time in a minute
Now it's five
Thirty eight years to plant a flag!
To leave the exist at youths heeded approval and become a man

Bound

Highly commended, Pride and Diversity Poetry Competition

My chest
My tits
My breasts
My over sized glands
My ripe hurting war wounds
Heavy like anchors
Weighing my ship down
Stopping me from leaving the dock
From sailing free
Bound by day in isolation
Unleashed as night draws in
Now raw, heavy, alien
Swinging loose in a storm
No use to me
Just agony
Of what could be
Without them
I would be free to set sail on my journey

Books

I am on the divide
between
places you want to be and places you don't want to see
A border of hope and past caring
As if this is how I always lived
Between
Growing old in the shadows of someone else's story
I was born female
Only at night would I take the fee and count it
Did I notice I had been short-changed?
I was male
Each night being told a bedtime story
Where I was supposed to be the princess

How can I rewrite history?
When the future sits in a cell
While the present reminds me nothing's changed
Till my mum sent me in a book
First published in 1984
A book where you are the hero
Where you choose who you are

That's when I understood the next page
Was my journey

The Argument

I just don't understand
Who dealt out this horrible hand
I sit soaked in sweat
In a cell dwelling in past tense
I am told I am a menace
What I bring to prison is simply a new tenant
Newspaper articles on too much leniency
Society is apparently keeping us out of villainy
Where just the dust through a culture with its filters on
Offend or pretend

Transgender prisoners are the hot topic
Torn apart by systems who care about what they look like
Transferred from male to female or female to male prisons
Do tell, say the prison bells,
What estate were you born to?

Sit soaked in sweat
While a room full of women debate
Only repeating ideologies from *The Sun*
On men who prey
Not who wear tears on the inside
Hide fears folded in body parts
Hearts forgotten
Too many used as cannon fodder in the news
The room rumbles then raises like red flares

I sit in the corner, ashamed that I haven't said a word
'We don't want their kind here. When are they getting shipped here?'
I look at my hands, try to figure where I stand
Then the patrol turns up
My induction is done
one transgender diversity rep leaving the room

Transgender Offender

Is it hard
Why can't you see me?
I shout my name
But you stare blankly
I walk among you every day
But you can't see me
Just a blurred reflection
Not me at all
Harp the violins, you breath
When made to address what you don't believe
for what I see when I look at me
My mirror as I stand
Pushing out, flattening, expanding on what I already have
My dreams are hard to see inside these walls
My needs look back at me like the glint in barbwire
Like hungry wolves they claw their way
Back out my chest
The rest is but a shadow
You don't quite place

Power, Privilege and Pride

Do you feel you need to hide?
Is true identity too hard to find?
Experience based on the society you were born into
You surrender to power and privilege
But where's the pride?

Don't be silenced
What happened? What's important? What's avoided?
Speak out!
Gender, race, sexuality or age
Does religion or class seal your fate?
Behind all that is denied
Behind pre judged notions
Is a heart

Knocking down barriers
To be spoken to directly, rather than the person next to me
Or not to fear interactions with anyone due to my gender identity
To walk into a bathroom and not be assaulted
My validity not judged by if I pass well in society
Or not checking where I can take holidays
in case I am breaking a law
To not go hungry or homeless
Or worry about what message my wardrobe is sending out
To be expected to change my name upon marriage
or questioned if I don't

I simply want to be seen as me

Destiny

In all my nightmares
Where demons dared to tread
Sweat crept across my body
Holding me down like vines
Intertwined with cement

Back then, I saw life through tinted black windows
Where are my friends then?

Ten become two
Who knew
What years separated friends from me
Snap them off
One by one
Like branches from a tree

Who could forgive me
Behind black tinted windows
I travelled in my own self made tomb
To a destination my nightmares could not even picture
A place of hate and pain
Lost in echoes of past mistakes
To late I had found my fate
From our first date
Your love shielded me like angel's wings to my destiny

Monsters

I am sweating. Fears branches scrapes windows. Claws grow
sharper. Conjure thunder. There in the dark. I sit waiting. My mind
manages to conquer breath. Slower. Slowing. Slow. Listening. Clock
ticking. Creek. Miss a beat. Fear grips my chest, tightening each rib
with nuts and bolts till I become Frankenstein. Open my mouth, fall
into an oyster shell. I am drowning. Those dark corners alter my
perseption. Slaughter innocence with anger. Leather straps to silence
screams. While monsters play. Mother leaves. Between day break
and youth. To barristers reading police notes. I choke back the
monsters tongue. Close my eyes, so I can't see what I have done. I
become a shadow, a sound of breathing forming mist. Sat in a cell.
Locked in a room. Clock stopped at noon. Wondering what the
monsters fear? Across a sea of bolts secures and peepholes hold
dreams. Everyone here is someone's monster. Now my friends.
When I stretch out a leg into the dark of nothing. I release it was me
all along.

Prisoner-Led Inductions

'I'm here to do inductions.'
Disruptions as my introduction is met with a tannoy
"Miss Smith to the office."
Discussions flare as tension meets untrusting faces
"Yes I am going to begin, I am a diversity rep, Shannon trust mentor
and listener."
Eruption from the loud mouth who's already been in
'I wrote this induction, been here, heard it all before, weren't you out
and come back in?"
"No that's you, I have been here all along, but isn't it good we have
someone who knows the score for all those who have not been in
before, so who's a first timer?"
Tall girl in the corner looks down at the floor
A girl so deep in her chair nods at me
with eyes that look like fishbowls
Another girl's face wild eyed and bruised
looks at her and nods 'me too'
The connection is met with a look that's half a curl from a smile
"Right, let's start."

The Jigsaw Maker

Koestler awarded certificate

When you start out slowly in the world
Eyes gaze on silently
Holding in breath
Nodding at first then totally still
As you take your first steps
Baby steps, baby steps
Sometimes you wobble, fall, grip onto air
Little feet, little hands
In a world of mystery
How some things never truly change
Though the world around becomes smaller
Each day you take your baby steps
Encouraged to learn, to grow
Starting small, build up
All around you, by law all things divide
We sometimes never have that watching eye
Silently, gazing, nodding
Encouraging us to learn
To use our hands to build
Fit puzzles together
Piece by piece
To many of us
Never hear the words
Breathe
If at first you don't succeed try, try and try again
We're left to make that jigsaw un-aided
When the pieces don't fit we throw it away
Stamp on it, cry, lose the picture
So when it's time to return after the hurt
There's nothing left to start from
We build the corners
Hoping that one day
Where have an idea of the picture we started from
Till we smash it again and again
Till we end up here
Four walls, broken dreams
More time to think than anything

But then silently the jigsaw makers appear
Maybe through tears, through all your fears
That gilding hand
One piece at a time
The picture will come gradually back
One step
Baby steps
I'm here
The jigsaw maker
Fits it all back in
Slots pieces back together what once was lost
The jigsaw maker
The watchful eyes
The safe feeling you first try to hide
The reason you smile
There are no thank yous
Only misty eyes
The final picture complete

Education Reflections From Inside Out

Printed in closing ceremony booklet 2018

I in trusted in you
Written in the dust of all I know
Lined across blackness
Cell doors banging
A knowledge
This is all I have
Forgotten in this maze
My gregarious spirit
Seeks life beyond the bars of my soul
Thank you for giving me your wisdom and adding to my wealth
Of knowledge and belonging

Lost Acorns

HMP Low Newton Library winner of Holocaust Memorial Day.

We are all connected
Brought together
Through the power of words
From the moment we are born
The birth certificate is wrote on
A name
A map begins to form
A family tree grows up out of an acorn
Up, up
Out of the earth
From that day forth
A tree is born
Each branch another line in our past
As we move on
Higher and higher
All reaching up to the sky
Millions, billions spread out across the world
We are all people
We all beat life around our bodies

THE BOY BEHIND THE WALL by Dalton Harrison

We are all searching, learning
Trying to make a history of our own
The only problem with that power
Is when one person uses theirs to change the world
In their mistakes we need to remember
We are all just acorns
Trying to rise up out of the earth

Walk In My Shoes

Outstanding work certificate, Walk In My Shoes Competition

I am a travelling salesman
I sell broken hearts and disappointment
I specialise in lost dreams
Check my book, it's written in black and white
I am often cavalier in approach
Smiling like nothing's wrong
But I choke
Once every day is done
I look at my catalogue
Of visions, of decisions
I wish I never made
Each in plastic slips of regret
Sold to me
So I can resell it on in pain
Double my accounts
While I carry on living my life in shame
Tame me, contain me
Piece by piece
I find loose jigsaw puzzles to fit
No box to work from
I can't see the full picture
Until it hits me
I am my own worst enemy
One two, many felonies
left me on the inside
With nothing but time
No room to hide
Just me
You can walk in my shoes
But will you truly ever see my heart
Now I walk in prison shoes
Stare through bars
Look out over barbwire fences
I know my feet echo in my past mistakes
But it's never too late
To change my destiny

Conflict

What in words
Can I define the role of us
The ones who have no idea
how to step between their ideas and reality
if any
My mind circles between psalm 23 and gangstas paradise
What makes my mind clean
one thing's clear
All I do is repeat past sins in my mind
Like that's all my mind can do is question me?
Is the valley of the shadow of death
Like the words I was made to repeat at school
for the charge of the light brigade?
Is all I was ever taught
Just a metaphor for me
to meet my fate
too late
From prison defined in dust and debris
conflict so ready
Where humanity is a heavy boot down the valley of corridors
Surely goodness and mercy will follow me?
Yet the ones we hurt remains to be seen
What I can't believe is how is cruelty going to save me?
When I leave here on foot
Or in the boot
Will this really change me?

Life Inside

My life in a word
Guilty
Nothing learned
Pockets of adventure
Dreams and fantasy
Distorted, lost, controlled
Phases
Just a phase
My life outside
Running along a blade till my shoes wore out
One door another
Another to you

Remembering back to childhood hopes
To have friends
To no longer be the one left out in the cold
A moment
A series of moments that lead me to your door
The sweatbox, heat, loss
The air slipping out of my pocket
The adventure just to see a cloud, a car,
all the things I took for granted on the outside
My life!
My inside life
Frosted mirrors of smudges, plastic
Dark corridors, closed doors
Voices whispering
Shouting, hate
Contorted faces behind shut gates

You open up my door
Tell me- who cares
You sit beside me
Laugh, all your fears remind me of my own
My friend
Don't forget how far we have come
From frosted windows and dark hopeless nights
Now it's your time to shine
Behind the other side of the looking glass
Your journey is just about to start

The Prison Path

I joined the Buddhist group in prison
My mission to use my time to find
My enlightenment
Although not quite the quiet of a monastery
Nor the retreat where you can leave
Smells do linger
Once shoes removed
That no incense stick can mask
Meditation to my safe space
Is often interrupted by alarms
Once eyes are opened
I am met with a commotion
As half of sewing sisters motion
From behind barred windows
Waving and winking
Pilot yoga brought to you in the gym
Asks you to relax and breathe in deeper through your core
More sniggers
As farts can't be ignored
Before someone shouts over
"I ain't closing my eyes, the room's full of criminals!"

Reception Listener

Duties to include
Making them a ready made meal or toast, a brew
While the officers wait on nurses
Take mugshots and do paperwork and curse us
I heard one shit themselves in the wagon
I heard one's drunk
While I sort out clear bags
1x prison greys
1x deodorant

Duties don't include
A smile, a kind word, an extra biscuit, a reassuring word,
a breakdown of what's to come
But I don't run the system
my job may not be salary bud I value it
My motto is do it right and that way they will remember
there is always a little humanity even in hell

Homeless

Those nameless
Could you be blameless?
Shameless?
For their dreamless eyes.
Those who are homeless-
Less than a home.
Told to only move on-
Who's to know.
What feelings pass those
Who often get passed
Under bridges
Given only a wide berth
No eye contact, no exchange

Yet as I sit waiting in reception
For those new additions
Who arrive on white wagons
Who's to say it's not a carriage?
A palace to those who never sit in public transport.
A lift. A ride. A nod, a voice.

We're here,
Like holidays some will never know.
A food bag on the other side.
Fresh water to those who may look for handouts.
You're in prison now.
These conditions make me stiffen.
But when they enter
I am only met with a peaceful smile.

One Man's Walk Is Another Man's Drive

As my chest breathes in like moving trees
My mind is enveloped like origami
As a child I first looked into the demon's eyes
With blind faith and innocence
Now lost even to myself
I am the heartbeat of consequence
Cut ridges cross patterned ridges
Youth's torn page
Age coming to hang me at dawn

I am lost or found?
some days I feel loved
others I am faced with old sounds of hate
wounds open up
infection seems to lay in wait
I am damaged
I am broken
I long for those childhood days
with demon's eyes looking through my father's silence
He knew I was waiting
He knew
I would become nothing
he hoped
Never hoped
if he ever even cared
But he saw what I see now
my eyes have demons
waiting
behind eyelids and blood
I am lost.
I am damaged.
but I have learnt to close my eyes whenever they come.

Particular Set Of Skills

You get into prison
Start to fit in.
Get to know those who have been in
Again and again
To those who never got out
Count what's left and what remains are the ones more in than out.
In prison you never get nowt some say you never get nowt for nowt
You look around and soon find out
Each person has a special skill set
Those who do crafts and can make you a card
Those who do weights are good to help with intimidating, if needed
Those who sew can sort out your clothes
Those who can write
have been known to pen a dirty letter to someone they don't know
for a price
Ex-solicitors reading files
Ex teachers be mentoring in maths, English and reading
While hairdressers use clippers on the wing and get extra canteen
Artists draw pictures for other people's children
Hidden cooks in the wing make do for birthday parties
While my particular skill sets
remain closely guarded for the after-party
I am hired for my famous slut drop

When The Door Is Locked

I get sick of my dreams
Like walking into the mist
Of my mind
Battlefield scared
Sword heavy
I wake in fits and starts
I sleep bent arms as if in prayer
Head tilted high as if the sky
Will appear before me
Not brick and mortar
Locks and bars
Designed to confine

My whispers in these hours
Are not there to ask
Not there to martyr me
In the words I now speak
Only I long for a sleep
That no longer echoes the past

The Gym

I love the gym
Full of din
Like old school halls
my chance to shoot hoops and kick balls
Watching people from my spot
You eye the risk-takers selling drugs to the other wings
Observe those who only come down to see their girlfriend
View the gym legends hitting weights deep in conversation
enjoying the competition
The hum of the lights
strip search when the officer comes
I consider the places people are stashing their goods
Music taking me back to when I worked the clubs
I look at those with the best trainers on
The latest leggings
A combination of perfect pull up hair and pull ups
Heart racing as you see your girl
Tabata workouts
The only place you can run without getting done
Where teamwork gives you goosebumps
But never play netball with a Slovakian!

The Time Traveller

I time travel
Unravel
Separate gravel with the red of bloody feet
Rattle castle doors locked for the likes of me
The hours I sat alone in a chapel
The moment my family was someone else's
while I just looked in

I time travel.
leaning against broken panels
Watching myself like the friends I will never have
trying to patch things up
Unskilled unknowing
what there was to unpick
after the damage is done

I time travel
back to novels not yet read.
not yet noticed like the dent in the wall with my imprint
Tackle the words as I watch them said in breath that has now left my
body
But I go back
I go back

I time travel to the past
Now my future like I am travelling trapped in a loop
Seeking what?
Seeing me
Baffled and alone

Now I travel and sit in the space of emptiness
A vacuum of no one
To repeat those moments I didn't see

Now I travel long hard roads
That looked worn as I travel back and forth
I am a time traveler
Rattled shackled grappling with so many battles
I have yet to win

One Day

I look back at the past
Like a broken record of thoughts
Lost in blink decisions
Visiting emotions like catapults
Breaking glass
The floor shines in shards like a sea of regret
At best
What remains are the holes

I know
I am ready to leave
This house I have built
Find a new street
Were the windows don't need to be boarded up
Where I can lock my door
Sit down and not have to jump up
Lingering on past issues
I carry them all in a rucksack of pain
Each boulder inside marks my desperation
Guilt, hate and shame
I listen as my chest mimics the patterns of the train
that comes past every night at this hour

I want to change
I'll start by showering
Reading a book and not crying in between the pages

Maybe one day this rucksack won't be so heavy to carry
That sometimes I could leave my cell without it
Count my newfound blessings and follow the sun
and not be afraid of getting burnt

Interlude

The last time I saw my mother's face
On cobbled streets, we silently embraced
Tasted salt on my lips, tingling in my fingertips
Hid my fear inside locked ribs
What fragile fragments framed
This is just an interlude I heard myself say
To finally pave the way
For now far from fortune's fresh day
Holding each other up in that moment in May
I never believed
In all those dreams that followed
This brief interlude
Bittersweet and tangible
Would leave me without you

A Giant's Breath

Darkness cradles my mind
Intoxicated demons rise
Out, out of my soul
Eating me whole

I search the night for peace
Yet all I see is flickering lights
All I hear is wind
The bang of my cell door
With each gust
Like a giant's breath
It hits me
Cold, stagnant, dead

I sit in the corner
Losing my heart to memories
I am but one echo in the dark
Flashing lights, hit and scatter across my wall
Like a projection of old home movies
I reel and recall as life slips away
But stillI hear the blood behind my ears
I hear the voice in my head screaming
The past like a jagged knife peeling back the layers

I lay here
Heart vs head
Blood vs brain
Love vs pain
I lay here
Knowing all I can do is lay here
Heart vs me

I hear life in the distance
Too far for me to touch
I could retrace my steps, but lost in a giant's breath
I can't find my way out again

Moeder

What harsh winds batter my window
My tears follow the streaks as my black eyes peek
On to snow soaked paths
Soft mounds of snow covering rough edges
With isolated patches framing my new world
Bright white to cover bars, to paint fences
and make barbwire look like candy floss
To follow morning
My mourning
My mother's fire awaits
To signal death in all its glory
Yet still I have seen the moonlight
Yet still the stars sat nearby
Yet still where the shadows dare to creep behind closed doors
I can hear music and laughter

I know there's still adventures to be had
I know there is still a future
I know I never thought all these things would be true
The day they told me you had gone
When I realised I had still got up
When I realized I had gone to work
When I realized I had gone listening
Before I knew all those things
Stuck rooted in all I hoped would never happen

I miss you
Yet still I hear your voice
What a beautiful sunrise
Yet still I hear the wind
Wet floors of concrete
Walls so far in front
Yet still I see the sky
The sky that shows me there's still a heaven
Heaven on clouds of colour
Where only birds can keep its secrets
Tearful beyond words
I wonder what they know
I hope in all that space
On heaven's wings there is only peace

Life

Silent seats
Handcuffed while looking out of windows
Past the gate
Feeling like Dorothy
As the colour gets switched on
Travelling on real streets
Real people
Stood at bus stops, walking or riding a bike
Real people
Normal people
My heart is lost between knowing this exists
While feeling I do not

The Funeral

Lost faces go home
Prelude to the interlude
Final farewells said

A Mother's Love

Written by me, read out by the Baptist minister at my mum's funeral.

Through silent child's eyes
Lie oceans of rippling tides
Blankets of stars reflecting
Across the water's edge to eternity

Through a child's eyes
The world is infinite
Thunderstorms of delight
Electrical storms of moonlight

Shining, guiding light
So bright
Only a mother's love
Can contain its embrace

Two Souls

Two lost and weary souls
Found each other
Behind barred windows and high fences
Lay vulnerable in time's icy grip
Sharing friendship, love while talking of what once was
The past streaking down windows
Racing clouds across the sky
High above rain falls, seasons change
Yet what remains
Two lost and weary souls
Found each other when the world shut the door
Behind it all
Time's icy grip hanging as the clock ticks
In the corner of the room

Prison Sleep

Nightmares tear me from sleep
It's midnight
Half of 12 is 6
6 the devil's number
666
I trace the wall
Midnight
Nightmares still grip me
Thoughts just rip me from my slumber
$12 - 6 = 6, 12 - 6 = 6, 12 - 6 = 6$
666
The devil's arguments
$6 - 3 = 3$
The witching hour
Midnight's split me
If by law all things divide
Then my heart will surely halve
The day I leave you behind

Paper Aeroplanes

We all just paper aeroplanes
Flying on the wind
Whether it's fate that connects us
Tests us
As we glide fragile
Yet so defined
On pockets of air and trust
Hitting high
Hitting low
But in the end we don't really know
Where we are going to go

We can fly side by side
Sharing the same current
Hurry on by
Fly, fly, fly
Till one of us drops
Streaming notes in the sky

It's never goodbye
We're all just paper aeroplanes in the sky
Till it's my turn to glide by
For a while
But I'll never stop writing
I love you in the sky

Shadows On My Wall

I've always loved the sea
Memories change and circle
Hurt, dreams whirl inside
Glide along, white foam, repeat
Hear nothing but sounds
Salt in the air
Wave after wave

I've always loved the sea
Kneel down on hot sand
Land that goes on and on
No walls, fences or bars
Hard just staring at a picture
Mixture of feelings
Overlap
Trapped
Repeat
Like the waves to the shore

One day, one year
The sounds, the air, the roar
The tide will change
Lace my lungs with freedoms breath
I'll sit and watch the waves
No longer just a picture on my wall

Echoes

I sit alone behind doors, barrs, fences
Society's defences
For all the wrongs I can't make right
Tiny lights flicker behind hundreds of closed doors
Enclosed tombs, human vaults
Society's defences
Against each and every one of us
I see these lights
Hear the rain outside fall
For now the only sound that proves my existence is my heart
Beating in time with the rain drops
No more screaming
No more jurisdiction
Until unlock or roll call
Heavy footsteps crunch floors
Patrol state
The lyricism of life inside with echo

Signposts

I am leaving footprints
in prints and I wonder why I slip in the mud
I am signposted like signal boxes
One way tracks so I never divert
from planned journeys on a tube map
Detached I learn in the third person about coercive control
how it takes its toll

I split my life
into three chapters and the past repeats regardless
until I found myself inside

What's your red flag?
What's your triggers?
flinching I never knew
I had spent my life sleeping with a loaded gun
decisions, consequence, reflect detect
I see patterns form in mind maps following maze after maze
never reaching the middle or the end

I am inside because outside is not my home
but when I get out
I need to rip the shadows off the wall
form shapes so I can walk
build dreams from clouds
I see over fences that trap me here
I need to find the hope and tears
my mum gave to me when I was born
that I gave back to her on our final call
I need to breathe and start to move forward

Containment

Two years of my life in multi-coloured texture
Telling me I'm not fit to live in society
White plastic lumps of cut-in trauma mark my walls
My brickwork dirty and decaying
Singe the dust
The matter of particles left by those who no longer share this space
how easy I fit in it
How quick DNA fragments are marked down to broken
No crime committed here
No time to fill in paperwork
Plaster cracks sand down bumps file over the scars
Undo the tape
not much of a scene
When all said and done, what's the texture of me?

Suddenly

The world wasn't ready for what I had to tell it
The voice inside, nailed my mouth shut
Too tough to talk to the outside
I felt so alone
The clocks went back, the clocks moved forward
I stayed lost in these hours
It was there I grew in the dark, kept quiet
So I didn't get noticed
I pulled myself inside out
Denied all I knew even to myself
Till all that was left was you

I lied, cheated and stole
To keep the demons at bay
Yet all I found was further pain
Four walls and metal frames
Detained in a lifetime's regret
Dissociation in a night that had many personalities
Written on the walls was words someone else wrote for me
Is this a dream?
Suddenly the clocks went forward and I am free

Tomorrow

My yesterday was locked in the years of solitude,
The chaos of best-laid plans put to rest,
Finally,
My today was not its best,
Left instead to a larger memory of could-haves,
No I'm still inside, still waiting for life to start,
My tomorrow way off
My tomorrow changes daily
Like my yesterday in years, tears, hopes and dreams,

I hope tomorrow brings you to me,
Yet another day closer
To you and me
A calendar reminder of what could have been,
My faith is slightly keyed
Even still
Tomorrow is a new day

Peer Mentoring

I found inside you develop skills
Not always seen by officers or OMU workers
Probation who remain on the outskirts
Remind us
'You're only doing this because you're inside.'

Exclusionary practice
So many missed chances with peer mentoring
Passed back and forth like pawns
Core complexities
Try not to summarise
Dehumanize people as just prisoners
As nothing more than piles of paperwork in offices
Just chapters in an ongoing narrative
Risk assessments, mental health records
Just prisoners
Just tension and nuances

Beside growing academic interest in prison life
Supporting little evidence of real change inside
The process is clear
Focus on funding
Use keywords
Where are the outcomes?
I feel disenfranchised
I want to be recognized for the work I do in here
That should be transferable on release
Not met with *what's that got to do with out here.*

Plant Killer

I was given red band privileges
Made to wear a band
that looked more like a garter on my arm
Transformed silent cells to whistles and winks
as faces pressed against bars
Allowed to walk where no other prisoner could go
Unsupervised
My job in gardens to water on weekends
Sends officers to radio their friends
"Don't think you're allowed in here?
Are you lying?
Why would they call it the sterile area
if you let prisoners in?"
I grin, tilt my chin
Pulling the long hose pipe to the gate
"Didn't they tell you sir, they hand picked me
as I was the only one who they knew,
the hose would not support my weight.
So I couldn't use it to escape."
Then he shrugged and opened the gate

One month to that date
I was let out late
Scorched all the plants in the greenhouse
Come Monday morning
Walking to education
A lifer screamed from behind the garden department
Ran rattling at the rail fence
"You killer! You killed them all!"
I felt a shiver filter down
"You weren't satisfied with just one! You murderer!"
The officer heard her and raised an eyebrow
While others, wide-eyed, stepped out the way
Making a byway
First in line
The officer found my name
"I'm innocent," I proclaim.
She exhaled.
"That's what they all say."

First Day On The Job

"You're going to be painting the landing, can you handle it?"
"I admit I am unfit but I'll give it a go."
"We don't do second coats, budgets don't stretch that far."
"But the sidebar needed doing twice
and the horizontal bar got scuffed."
"Rumours are you're getting fired."

First day as a wing cleaner
Heading over to detox
"Count your equipment, you are responsible,
rubber gloves can be used to fake drug tests."
I puff out my chest, nod my head
Led to a cell
One girl had slept in
She had smoked Buscopan
Over night, seemed more like weeks
When I looked at the sheets
I turn around and all my stuff's gone
Not long after the Scottish one
Tells me she the only wing cleaner who does detox
As she deals the drugs

First day on the job
' Gym orderlies clean and do workouts.'
I stay behind workout with the under 25's
"You gonna black out, you' re too fat to work out!"
"It takes all sizes to encourage better lifestyle choices."

First day on the job in education
A woman launches across a table
First day in BICs cleaning
one sits in the corner out of her head and yawning.
Later floods the machine and nearly runs over the cable.

First day of listening
after training sessions by the Samaritans.
Open my eyes to redefine myself
and what I am working for.
This is the first day I feel like me.

The System

I am shackled,
Made to feel less than human,
The shadows mimic movements,
But they are mocking me,
I am currently formless,
I am suddenly voiceless,
my face, like me is forgotten,
No image reflects back in smudged scratched plastic,
Hate-fuelled enabling environments
Justice served in a system of care leavers, beaten women, addicts,
sex workers abused fill criminology students' case files,
Designed to build a suitable system to house us,
Use words like depraved, vile, evil,
That and leave us to wet ourselves in transport wagons that secure us
For public safety,
For the public's best interest is to make me feel inhuman,
To make me stifle my cries of fear of using up too much oxygen,
To lock me in one-way-seen rooms
to leave out air because that's for the free!
To treat me like cattle to the slaughter,
 Numbered, tagged and delivered is my favourite bedtime story,

I am one!
Of a percentage that managed to live,
Line my mind with charts,
Pretty colours don't reflect much!
In the system is only dead babies and blood stains,
screaming echoes and buzz words,
Years of alarms and code blues code reds,
Twisted up to the seg,
No room for real issues,
just wait till you get out!
Ex-offenders are where the story starts.

When Battle's Done

Softly lit rooms
Echoing the only silence these four walls can bring
Nightmares glaze over lonely sleepers
As they fall, fall from grace
Fall from destiny
But a white noise to society
Time ceases in these moments of breathing in
The wood pigeon still coos
The light cracks across the horizon
Marking the dawn's call
Like the sound of soldiers slowly walking home

Two Years

Two years and here I am
730 days
I sit in reception
The room stinks of depression
The four girls around me
One in a wheelchair has family
One to the right is declaring herself homeless to York council
The one in the wheelchair lifts up half a leg
Underneath some pills they all rub their hands with glee
They know not to ask me
How funny it is to know everyone's eccentricities
Yet know nothing
Like married couples who pass and note every behaviour
but are past caring

Two years
730 days
As I look down at the £46 discharge grant
I will put it toward my rent in the hostel
The other girl laughs she getting Kinder eggs and condoms
'I will be in by next week, make some money,
be back with my girl, she's my only family.'
My girlfriend appears as she works in reception
I grab her face and kiss her until the others shout
'Come on, for fuck's sake man, we're getting out!'

The air is all I want to breathe
The air on the other side of that gate
I take a deep breath and all I smell is fags

Two years
730 days
I feel like I just left Doc Brown
The future's not what I expected somehow
Jump on the train with the girl whose tablets just kicked in
I shout as we pull out
A cathedral!
Cows, sheep!
'Shut up, you're embarrassing me!'

The trolley comes down the aisle
'Who this bitch thinks she is, she's staring.
I'll knock her clean out!'
'Calm down, that's how outside people look.'

We let her pass as I try to nod
But my smile loses its colour like the face of the girl
'You gonna be ok? Take a breath and sit on a bench.'
'Got to be ok, ain't no one else gonna help me,
once I'm packing and back in. I'll be sorted.'
I just hope she doesn't die
as I help her get off, we say goodbye,
I feel fear hit my ribs like a kidney punch
I try to think instead of worry
I am alone

Two years
730 days
Never even being able to walk and open a door
I make a list of all the things my girlfriend told me I need to do
Hostel, rent, I.D, bank, benefits, doctors
I wish someone had come to help me
All I got was my OMU getting me to sign my licence
2 years
730 days
and I am here

Between Words And Walls

Between the space
I left on leaving
You stood rooted in trust and envy, happiness and tears
My sentence just a two-year gap in my history
You rested your hands on brick
Our words the echo of my footsteps as they left with me
You stood rooted in the vines of a system
that believes it's always right
While you know
Too many miscarriages of justice
Hold the system up
We both hang on to this moment
A kiss for luck

In the still

Written in Becky Cherriman's class in the hostel

After the gates locked
After the last bell sounded
I felt a different breeze
One from behind the barbwire
One I had looked over fences to see

In the still
I stood
vexed, perplexed

Still, so still
I stood and shook
Your warm embrace still imprinted
The kisses still wet with my tears
I stood in the still
Feeling air surround me

I stood in the still of a morning just beginning
I whispered, under breath and foot
" I will be back for you, my love."
While the still waited to swallow me up.

Arrived

Written in the hostel in Becky Cherriman's class

Release day arrived
Derived from paperwork
Stamped on by officials
I will never know
Who tell me, I am unsafe
Until this date
To walk among the world

Hurdles leaped
Deep in bars and steel
Lock and key
Cuffed, shut in small rooms like tombs
Suffocating in silent screams
Nothing but barbwire glinting
displayed, sentenced, guilty

Release date's arrived
No more denial
Open the doors
You've settled your score
Only I never knew
How much barbwire slices
How much bars trap
That once you're let out
It follows you
Warning all others
Look, look
Surrounded in halos freedom
My own self-made prison

When You're Still There But I Am Here

I loved what we had before
I have loved everything in-between
but every minute I get to talk to you
I appreciate it so much my love
I appreciate your laugh & how I can tell
you're smiling when you talk
I love the magic of you
it comes out my phone and fills my room like perfume

Uncaged

The birds fly,
Time is wings,
Air tearing through yesterday,
A song from heaven,
That's why birds sing,
So we never forget,
A world beyond fences,
A world behind words, wishes, wants,
So we never forget to look up!

The birds fly out and back,
Between the vision we see,
Our place, our spot,
They show us somewhere there is a door unlocked,
Yesterday's lesson
Is tomorrow's grand plan,
We blur, blue, yellow and white
Tomorrow is mine!
Tomorrow feels like time,
But one tomorrow will follow the other
and you will, one day,
be by my side.

On The Out

One week sees one death,

Two weeks sees four more recalls, someone OD on the floor,
eyes so glazed like an animal stuffed in a museum hall,

A month, a girl on my floor handcuffed
and screaming in a drunk rage,
she's pushed into a van, it's a dawn raid,
A stark warning to all those who question their place back on the out,
With celebratory liquid or pill treats to mark the occasion,

The week after I am met with spitting rage by the vagrant drug dealer
that recognizes I am from the same place,
some girl swopted a rock for her phone now she needs to pay,

The week after she's not going out
and I am left walking the long way,

A day off two months and she loaned out too much,
I see recall after recall and wonder how she hung on this long,
While rehabilitated shoplifters ask me
if I want these expensive aftershaves,

two months and a day,
I replay my friend's suicide
while the voices inside her mind leave only death to snatch her away,
I watch in a daze handfuls of absconds drift out like tides,
I bump into them casually
outside parks or pharmacies and jobcentres,
saying hi but looking worse for wear laughing,

But today's a tooth missing, weight loss and a black eye,
Drunk men standing nearby questioning my concerned voice,
three months and I hear they're back inside,

Doing fine just saying hi, remembering the outside
like distance memories of childhood dreams,
lost daydreams wondering how anyone makes it out there it's crazy,
while I try to remind myself that I'm doing ok,

THE BOY BEHIND THE WALL by Dalton Harrison

That five months is seen with clear eyes,
Not robbed in streets by random acts,
My face beat but strangely don't call the police,

I see six months without sitting in dark dirty dens
hidden by respectable street signs,
In rooms designed to take your youth, your money and your life,

I wonder in a year if some will have made it here
without using prison as respite,
without losing their life,
without paper licenses keeping them right,

I wonder if they stand and say,
On the out is better than in here
On the out is worth all my tears

Perceptions

I said I wanted to see trees
Fields of gold,
Untold stories of animals and people through history
A testimony to all that's past
That lasted on in the folds of green and earth

I wanted to be able to walk for miles
No bars to block
No officer to call roll check
Or standing in queues
Dinner, meds, showers or work movements

I wanted to walk till my legs ached
Till my heart raced
To see freedom in a way I never felt before steel encased me
Changed me

I wanted to walk till I couldn't talk
Get up that hill
Triumphant open a door to my time in the outside world

I gained this memory
On hostel entering
To be told to do a MDT
I can't hardly breathe
Sweat and jelly legs have hit me
Like a liquid cosh
I took the swab
No Slavia there, just everywhere else

But it's negative!
There, see!
We have to check randomly...

I'm smiling the walk of the free
Even if I'm not used to it
I walked I walked
Till I couldn't talk

The Room Of Unclaimed Things

There's a room
It looms out
Whenever I go near
Reminding me of lost tears spent
Fears of losing myself again

That room
Like tombs of cells
I left behind
Forgotten souls and bleeding hearts
Dying piece by piece
Behind cuffed wrists and peephole slits

That room downstairs
Like an unmarked grave of black prison bags and old teddies
Hung-up clothes like someone's still standing
hunched, decaying like corpses
Rotting, forgotten
Marking the stop of no return

In that room reserved for recalls
In that room for those who left unexpected
Of old ties severed
Of broken promises
Of solitude

It reminds me of all I was
When I close my eyes
I see the doorway open
To show me my darkest fears
To remind me of the devil inside

Strength In Remembering

My exit from the dock was swift
Floating, lost
Although the handcuffs sat heavy
I looked on them as if in passing
Catching the colour, the shine
Like trays of jewellery
resting peacefully in a Pandora shop
Alone I rose
Heard shouts from the gallery
I felt hazy like the moment your eyes flutter
on a warm day and you have been sitting for too long
I'm standing slowly, walking with anyone who feels the need to
follow
Like walking to town casually with friends
But now only me is left standing
Standing, standing, strong,
strolling into my sentence with a strength

I will remember this day and all the days that follow
I will remember
I stood up
I took it all in
Breathed in justice and breathed out me.

Taken

I wake
I breathe
before I ache
sharply as I take
The light
In my eyelids
The blinds tilt
In these small movements
I feel you
In conscious blinks

Deep in the dark of my brain
Detained in a prison
My shield
wrapped in skull
Red as my blood
As my love
My heart beating against bare ribs
Digs into my skin
Within carves
the hollow space
awaits your embrace
your place
a single pendant
My heart the locket
My dreams the key
only you
can open me

A Vagrant Society

Written in Becky Cherriman's class

To the world
Earl of manors
Spend flicking through media pages
Lazy eyed with coffee
Mornings dawning as frowns meet headlines
Define monsters and heroes on little dotted lines
Sentence, released, repeat
Re-invented ex-offenders back on the street
Labelled, cradling alien phones awkwardly
Walking around breathing in society's justice air
Bought and paid in taxes
and short changed by politicians and governments
These ex-offensive offenders walking around!
Some look at the ground, some look at the sky
The road ahead with not a closed door in sight!
Staring wide eyed at rotten teeth decaying men
Staggering with disease completely void of society
Who updates status after status
about ex-offenders walking the street.

Doodles

When I was small
Well say not too tall
Before life's doodles
Became the art of life
I would sit in low lit rooms
My heart beating like tiny drums
Like little hums
Doodling friends I did not have
Tracing love I had yet to find
Hiding tears of bullies
Fears of the future in my doodles
I found life like the roll of the dice
Not sure yet of what I would find.

Anything

Underneath the door is a light
So when I turn out the light I see it
long, stripped, outside my door lining the floor
As I lay in bed in the dark
In this dark
I am only me
In this silence that's all I see
My life in colourless shine
I could be ten again
I could be waiting for my mum to say good night
Goede nacht
In the dark before dawn
I could be anything

Freedom

I'm walking the street
On rainy hazy days
When buses come on time
So I'm left waiting on trains
Dark is rolling in
Schools kicking out
All noise, sirens and laddered tights
I'm feeling deflated
While specks of water hit my face
I search for nostalgia in charity shops
rather than coffee shops
When I have bills to pay
I feel empty like coffee cups
Lovers' lips still pressing
As we parted at prison gates
While I'm free to wait
No officer screaming
I can stop in stairways
loitering in society's background noise
No one stops to talk
I am free just to be on rainy days like these

Then I see a girl I used to know
walking unsteady
While her boyfriend vexes
she says sorry
You're nothing
Nothing but a useless girlfriend
always have been, always will be
He struts while she cowers
Maybe freedom's not the same for everyone.

Our Love

It's not in the loud bangs
I find love grips me
But in the soft sounds
After grief has sung its song
In that silence between
The last tear and a little smile
I find my heart darts
Carves your name on the edges of the air surrounding it
Sinking deep into the time that crowns it
What is love without a bridge?
That I can carry all these things
Between your heart and mine

You At The Back

The boy in the back of the class
Looks up at the wall but can't tell the time
Lies his way through lessons
Smiles silent in the right places
Traces in his mind the lines across trees outside
Sees seasons change
Sees his sense of ambition be blown out
like candles with each birthday
Every day's a workday
when you're two steps behind the crowd
Lock your mind away
It was never needed then
why start now?

Experience expands horizons
No view beyond
Getting smaller by the day
Walking on hot coals but accepting your fate
No change from being raised up
Till the frame clicks shut
A picture of you
Locked up

No room to cough
Forgot
Like boys in the back rows
Who know that's their place
Too afraid to engage
The boy behind the wall
Was always built this way
But inside locked doors
Needing more

Pressed faces against bars
Restricted and contradicted
Afflicted by the past
That lasts longer than the future

THE BOY BEHIND THE WALL by Dalton Harrison

One boy sits in a class
Reminding himself of all he's lost
Signs up for everything
Learns about how to unlock
A mind who can't see past barbwire
Now sees social poverty as a problem
Social capital as away to expand his potential
Motivation to write an essay of life on planets
Tectonic plates and dark matter
Does matter

Twenty X two = released into society
Time to change the minds
Of those who think
Prison education isn't worth funding

Rented Rooms

They say this room with its white walls and new carpet
I now rent once housed a smack head
The guy upstairs knew this to be true
Who now spits at me drunkenly
He knows this as fact as they had the same social worker

I think back to that time
I was still in prison
The smack head was still alive
Maybe the guy upstairs mouth didn't smell quite like rotting flesh
My mum was still laughing
Just living in bliss not realising that the cancer was waiting
Like I was waiting to get out
Like he was waiting to not wake up
Like that guy upstairs room mate had not yet been knifed
waited for that bus to take him there

For me to sit not knowing all these things to exist
now makes me grateful I'm alive
Makes me wonder how I made it this far

Ghosted

I stayed in all week
Maybe it was two
Who knew I had given up?
There was no trumpet call
Just quiet sobs and barricading behind closed doors
Only now I lock myself in
Never open blinds that line my window
Like the bars that lined my window where I came from
There is no one
No officer, no inmate, no hostel checks
Just me
Colours, patterns change inside this room
Draw shadows from my blinds against my wall
I see the graffiti that lines my mind
I am a ghost,
The system changes you from solid to liquid
no one listens
Officers look through you
Workers miss appointments
Ghosted from one prison to another
Overlooked, over criminal, over-stretched
The shadows leave me hot and sticky laughing in the dark
Once you're seen as criminal
you go from solid to fluid
The judge proved it
making me a sentence, a speech, irrelevant
Recorded and marked by lists and CCTV
But not humanity
Now I am ghosted from a hostel where they needed the room
To a bedsit that's worse than anything
Where the man upstairs sounds like he is dancing with the devil
The man below is paranoid I am out to get him
and is coming for me first
While the smell of weed washes like waves under my door
I can't fall when all I am is a ghost
only hope
When I wake from this dream
A battle on water towards barricades and screams
I will be someone everyone can see

Probation Meeting

What are you doing? Has anything changed?
Just needing to update my files,
we need to check because you're still high risk

What did I do last night?
I hid in my room
Listening to the drunks argue in many languages
With voices that only come out at night
These echoes flicker over the acoustics of my world

What did I do last night?
Listen to people kick rubbish
Gates creak as they open
Heard the sounds of plastic cider bottles flatten under cars
I crossed uncharted territories scrolling digital highways
Seeking life
Only what I got
Was a text from someone I used to know
That they had slit their wrists and throat
I rang our old hostel
as they would know her address to ring the ambulance

I nod as probation prompt,
Begin by talking about the job centre, then about my projects,
talk about still needing ID so I can access the things I need.

That's us all caught up was the reply
You know we can't help you with those things.
I will see you next week.

The Streets

In my street
Watch where your feet meet silver bottles, special brew and cider
On my street, poverty waves from every window
Graffiti is the jungle vines that covers all
Watching people stalk their prey with claw hammers
Because on my street you don't go out after dark
don't have flowers or they'll get trod on
See mattresses on corners
Like prostitutes coming home
See crisp packets stuck to human shit on curbs
So I walk in the road
On my street you don't clap for the NHS
so I stood behind blinds
Hidden with the lights out
So the police don't bang on my window
Looking, looking for someone
I am alone in human rubble
Like a war zone
Tone deaf play music on social change
No sign here
hip hop
Along the cracks on the floor
I didn't come from a street
Quite this bleak
But what's left after prison
Is what I see in front of me

Start Again After Starting Again

Past the Beeston barbers
dodge shit on route toward Beeston newsagent
too many b's in one place
nearly got run over by a white van but he lets me cross anyway
listening in to other people phone conversation
but only cos they start with fuck
young girls prance with glitter covered iPhone cases
talk about Aunt Wendy as they try to look older but walk too fast
I let them pass blowing smoke like the cars they cross to Co-op
I walk on I see echoes of the past like barbwire
Children's toys litter the gutter
signs saying *do not enter security in operation*
I think back to us
feel love at every corner
feel your breath on my neck when I run to catch a bus
force myself not to look again
as I catch reflections in windows:
what's worse than seeing you there?
Maybe turning round and seeing you're not

I long for hands to hold, not empty pockets
I want to get lost in your eyes, not my screen lit images
that linger on wishes of incoming caller and I want to cry
divide my time even out reality and fantasy
guess we're both doing time
but I'll walk that line if it leads me to you every time

Last Call

Let me carry your thoughts beyond grey walls
Colourless dull
Were grey t-shirts line wardrobes
No colour my lover
But love
My love's red carpet
My voice lined by clicks in the line
My smile creased by words
Turned up in the corners
As I say goodnight

Tastes Like City Life

I hit the town
This town of cigarette smoke
That I breathe in
Taste of a lifetime of regret
Watch men in tight t-shirts swagger
while the football win
lines the echoes of rain washing away the sin

My Days

My days always start with a love letter
But end in a suicide note
Choking words of wisdom
Hoping someone will listen
I sit in silence
that was once filled with uniforms and shrill alarms
Dirty cells with envelope mattresses
Between noise and silence
I become deaf
My days regard me knowingly
My days witness my signature
Pattern my paper
To write that letter

Probation

Some guy's stood outside, having a fag
Hoodrich hoodie on show
I look his way and he turns his back while flicking on his phone
Where reputation is currency he talks the talk
I don't feel the same as he rubs his shaven head

My situation is lined with frustration
Now incarceration is done
I have found new gatekeepers hold the keys to my new world
I risk recall if I don't fit in to what they want
I walk in like a mark has been burned on my soles
I feel the segregation between me and probation
Like I am a mutation
A mere citation on the end of their footnotes

This level of accusation and humiliation just tests my patience
Where the others in the waiting room look at me
like I am not one of them
While the ones behind the screen look at me
like I am a threat to humanity.

London Kings Cross

People calling out
Moving so fast like cars on a track
Voices echo and pass
Afternoon but the sun is still bright
People are always moving like a hive
Only tramps have time to sit
Blue skies across landmarks
High buildings covered in flags
like a circus tent above us all
so rich and alive
It feels like the buzz inside a radio
Each part alive in electric currents
ready to shock you if you get too close

I am alone
On streets I never thought I would see again
Carrying with me those I love
like I am showing them through my eyes
My journey, my life
I am visiting like a ghost from my past
Viewing the world like a stranger
I feel lost inside a universe too big for me now

Introspection

I spend my weekends making soup
My mind torn like the bread I dip
Skirting round the edges
I imagine this is what it feels to be human
Instead of nefarious
I have escaped the abyss of prison to probation
My life is no different
I was born with a life sentence
Born chained to other people's perceptions
Born out of darkness
To see light as just the shadows on my cell wall
Small bursts of serendipity
Fall like stars from the night sky
Both terrifying and ineffable in the depth of my soul

Solitude was the hand to rock my cradle
Oblivion the song that sang me to sleep
Sweet release
I look for redemption in each aurora
A quiver in hope's first light
Time has no meaning inside
Outside I find the true crime
Is time chimes the same

As my soup is nearly ready
I stir the pot
I look out the window
Thoughts sonder in each person below
I see my mother's face
My promise to make soup
Too late
I would be there
I would chop garlic
I would cut onions
Pretending I wasn't crying over the cancer
Over our lost dreams
I would cook tomatoes
Like our epiphany was yet to come

I would hear you you again mum, mellifluous
Speaking in her born tongue
'*Mooi, Mooi, lekker.*'
As I eat the soup
I taste *heimwee*
I swallow *tehuis*
I cry *moeder.*

Alone

I woke up within the hours
That neighbours would protest at my feet walking
The echoes of my mind now alive as I woke myself laughing
My dreams constant perseverance to partition the past
Diluted to make me laugh
Leaving out the burden
The business like blackmail
As reality sets in and I lay here
Thinking of all that has gone
Before moments become anecdotes
We tell ourselves

Home For Christmas

I see clouds spread like outreached arms
Trees grow out of marshlands raised out of dirt
Shiny man-made landscapes
Mixing with the earth
Roads bridges paths tracks
Traveling moving till one day we stop
Divided in barbwire fields
following mud and hedges, blood and history
The wind walking carrier bags like Scottish Highland terriers
Flocks of seagulls holiday further inshore
Sheep, alpaca and horses eating from the same bucket
share stories of animal farm
or is it the season of goodwill? I'm not sure
Deers play in the dirt jump and thump unaware of my train
Rain hits my windowpane
I'm travelling home for Christmas
Where the barbwire divides children from family
Where the high walls and gates hide
Christmas time inside
Where my love waits for me
Christmas Eve kisses without the mistletoe and wine
Yet all I need is your smile

Untold Christmas

I'm waiting on trains
Displayed, delayed then cancelled
it's Christmas Eve
Security cleared kisses passed in the visitors' hall
next time I see you it's the new year and I'm forty
Right now it feels
Like everyone frozen to this platform in Durham
wishes they were not
but I am here grinning with all I got
from those hours brief and tamed
watched by officers
To me a table full of Christmas morning

Nightmares

In-between the sheets
I find tangled between now and dawn all my regrets,
Like knots in my back,
I circle my own body like buzzards waiting for death,
Hexed to what if's
Vexed in my mind in decisions made in my name,
I can only weep in mocking thoughts like crowds jeering,
Spitting at me like sport,
I see the shadow of these mistakes
creeping across my wall like ghosts,
 unable to rest in any life but their own,
I see the bars stripped in lines
as they walk and spin to turn
as the room grows that bit smaller,
I see the light come through the blinds
it's here between it all,
I speak to my father,
Like no time or pain has ever entered our lives,
it's here we all live like a family that was never torn in half,
I take the pain like it's displayed in shop windows
with a tag price of reduced as I lose myself in this,

I blink at the dawn,
That light that has weaved the pattern of my sheets,
A mosaic of life,
In all the nights like this,
Am I running through somebody else's walls?
Inside their nightmares?
Do I meet them and have to dwell in their night times vision of hell?
Unable to dream in both,
I am where night makes it bed
All torn sheets with the scent of decay
This fear inside night's grip,
To treat deep,

To walk in my dreams is to know what it feels like to see death,
In the chokes of a lover's hand around your neck,
Hating the world inside your slowly lifeless eyes,

THE BOY BEHIND THE WALL by Dalton Harrison

I am the product of a father's rage and a mother's wish,
I am a mirror of his anger in a cloak of all her tears
I am buried in the aches and pains of their life,
To burn in the smoke of their lost screams,
I rise out of smolder,
Out of ash and black with wrath,
Compare my despair,
With my father's hate and my mother's broken dreams,
Shattered like glass around the hands that point at her,
My father, my demon,
The seed I grew from to make me,
but my reflection now only shows me,
I confuse the clicks in my neck with the bolts turning in prison doors,
I hear the fury of past echoes,
The slow, deep knocking of my enemies at the door.

The Prison Dreams

Inspired by Jackie Kay's Poem No 115: Dreams in the class with
Amanda Dalton and Mary Colson with the Royal Literary Fund
while returning to hostel for a class

The gates hate new visitors and cold callers
The vans choke and splutter impatiently waiting
The tall slender fences wink at passing motorists
While floodlights warn winter walkers to hurry home
Bars brace themselves against the cold
Denying access to those whose name not down
Reception is embarrassed by the mess
They weren't expecting visitors so late
Secretly feeling guilty they have nothing in
The officers' office checks the time,
eavesdropping and taking notes:
'Better watch this one!'
The corridor ignores everyone
Remaining transfixed by its shiny sheen
The induction wing stops watching telly
As a fight breaks out in detox
Who is too busy joking with segregation
'That's another one down the block.'
Dining hall is wishing healthcare would call in
as last night's curry is still repeating
While the education department talks
about current affairs with the long-term wing
The gym's sweating out all its sexual frustration
Nearby the Chapel is offering a safe space
Just across the visits room is raising an exhausted eyebrow
to private visits, who shrugs,
Overhearing all about last night's phone call
and how David's not shown up
The other wings hoot and holla
between the slits and cracks lining the prison walls
The cells hide from them as their bullies
as they relive their regrets silently
The CCTV hopes the public does not hear about this
and turns away
from the corners called hate, hope and dying

THE BOY BEHIND THE WALL by Dalton Harrison

The locks continue to whisper,
'They're out again.'
As benevolent listeners shake the sleep from their eyes

The prison stares back and forth like a parent
trying to unsee the carnage of sibling ferocity
Finally sits back in a moment's reflection
and dreams along with the garden department
about rolling waves and sun drenched beaches

The Ex-Poet

You may wonder
Why I still rhyme about doing time
But the system does not fit the crime
Too many are sent in line
As society's cannon fodder
Like an unwritten rule
A culture bias
Too tired to correct its leanings
Teasing baby boomers,
appeasing generation X
Cultures built on mistakes
Are merely left to feed
the hungry media millennials
To sell rights to a franchise
to finance a government's unjust tyranny
I have felt the iron hand of its justice system
Behind the dead eyes of those who can't talk
With ligature marks around their neck

When I left I promised myself
I was not just every mistake I ever made
Even still I cry
I am the best and worst of humanity
my tears of shame will never bring back my innocence
As I wonder what I deserve in line with the rest of this world

What am I?
I whisper into closed blinds
That look like bars on my wall at night
Ex-villain
Ex-offender
Ex-female
Ex-poet
Who is devoted to the spoken word of life

With The Caps On

Written,
Unwritten,
Spoken,
unspoken
If thoughts were weapons
Used in words
we would choke.
In letters and capitals
Too big to swallow
We would fill pages
That turn to water in our hands
Surely we would drown?
When one person's journey is an exclusion zone.
The other is a cell no bigger than a box.
Who gets to tick the boxes?
Highlight male, female.
Am I another?
I am a dream of being me,
In all the screams,
who looks at
my safe space and how it's threatened by hypocrisy?

Media Friendly

You tell us we can move on
You say we done our time
Yet all the while
You line our coffins with the brimstone
from society's righteous fire

You tell in certain cycles
How well we done with pride
How the job of some has rehabilitated
the worst of the worst this time
You say it so assured
While you line our coffins with brimstone
from society's righteous fire

You feed the media paranoias
You gather and twist open old files
You unlock old media footage
While lining your pockets with victims' old letters
You put the sort code on the past
You feed the entertainment wheel
You spin it to win it
You tell us we are not our worst mistake
While you line our coffins with brimstone
from society's righteous fire

You don't care what's right or wrong
As long as it's prime time

Desolate

I spend the morning picking away at skin
ridding myself of all the sin
the mind pops bubbles
replaces words with air
that crackle and spit like fire
I circle around dream in a word search
only to wonder where my dreams went before I pulled them out
like a picture a child shows his mother
only to be reminded she's now dead
memories removed
I face the mirror, as if fate has taught me,
red is the colour to all my decisions
My legacy of collisions
Conditioned, repetition
now it's time to be mindful
youth has left with the door firmly slammed
Circle a word search
dredging
conscious
solace

My Home

When the door's left unlocked
Bells and shouts lurk in places I try to forget
The sound of fresh buttered toast is only a few steps away
But I am framed in a picture of past mistakes
I'm locked in my blanket
I'm fighting with the tangled mess
Of the mind map now spreading in my head
I'm bolted burned branded into the folds of sheets
Denting them with my feet
As I try to find release
As I try to unlock my dreams
I am listening to rain battering my window pane
The dark is looming
Cloak and dagger weaving
slowly leaving footprints across my body
while the draught blows the top layer off my chalk lines

I wonder if they found me here
how they would describe me
Isn't the narrative of my life forever in past tense anyway?
Is fear behind my door
Or my brain contained like cctv
recording my vision of decisions
learning how to keep me here longer
tired tears tearing at the sheets
looking for an escape in the shape I once left

Visit Day

I sat in yards
On stony ground
With the grit of officers boots of prisoners who left
Their dust behind
I saw the imprint as my hands moved up from leaning
I saw lines traveling
While I stood still
In yards designed to keep me here
I traced clouds for years
But they never matched the shape of clouds beyond the walls
Like the barbwire had cut them in tatters
Out here the clouds are free like me
as I travel with them behind train windows
I came back to where it started
to see you and kiss you my lover

I Miss You

You ask me if I miss you?
I simply smile
While the phone line hides
The miles
I miss you enough to fill
The empty space in our bed
With a hot water bottle
So all that is between us will never grow cold

My Time

I still lie crumpled like bed sheets
Day after day
Like a Tate award called
Unmarked grave
I'm still waiting
I'm still over thinking, overwhelmed
I'm still, so still,
I could be a statue
Birds would swoop down and rest on me
Lovers would use me as a marker
to meet for first dates or coffee
I'm still frozen melting in places
Lost like the polar ice caps
Just drifting away
On days like this
I do nothing
Am tussling with me
My mental memorial service
Of days weeks years lost
A list of unfollowing what I made
A play of my life
Only for everyone to walk out before the end
I'm still, I'm still
Like I'm reliving birthday parties where I had to win musical statues
Like I'm hiding behind sofas seeing my first horror movie,
Only now it's not a movie, it's my life
Making me rooted, my mind's tooled up, deaf to conclusions
Scared of delusions
I'm still like soaked bed sheets drying harder
I'm still wishing the ghosts would stop passing through my walls
I'm still,
working on it

Sinful

I wanted to tell myself it was ok
Yet in the dark of youth's uncharted map
I heard my parents say
Lying is sinful
continually I tried to deny I even did it
Lying here
To cover guilt
small but under the surface it bubbled up
No I needed to lie more
Then design a way to remove the lies to leave myself free
But these lies would never truly hide me
I was the lie to hide behind my parents' mistrust of anyone like me
I was the original sin born out of good intentions
but grew out of shape in my own skin
I needed to blend in
but the lies only circled the board in a family game of frustration
I felt nothing but hate and white hot rage for my situation
played monopoly and ended up in jail
looking back now I hated me for hating me
for never having had the guts to say this is me
yet here I stand with no one left to tell
I'm no longer lying, not even to myself
yet in that echo I wonder if it carries
on angel wings to my mother's resting place
just so I can finally say *are you proud of me?*

Stranger

I walk through streets
Past the mud of motorbikes skidding.
Into the park
Where the tracks follow me
I walk past the Asda trolleys
Past the girls in the chipped concrete pen
Blasting music and exercising
Multi-racial scenes
Multi-layered in poverty

A slice divided on a chart in some council office
Overcrowded
Over-criminal
Over by the food bank the line meets the street I'm in
Past the walking dead already drunk
Past the shouts of *what you fucking done?*
Past the lives still growing
as mothers call

Five minutes left on the street play

Past the rubbish stuffed in alleyways
Past the sofa and the cabinet
Like the open side of a Wendy house
Past the take-out shops
Past the launderette with the door open
Heat of dryers blasting out into the street

Car fumes
Cigarette plumes
Kids kicking cans talking in whispers
Half-eaten boxes pigeons eat out of

Past the heads down
Past the *you got a cig mate?*
Past the feral cats who sprint
Past the bus stops with quilts underneath
Past the traffic going at speed

THE BOY BEHIND THE WALL by Dalton Harrison

Past the social club
into the park through a flooded metal barrier
Past the bench where the bin's kicked over
Past the dog walkers
Past my neighbours house with the old carpet rolled up
Pass and enter my door

Catch my face shining in pools of dirt
merely a silhouette of all that surrounds me

In time I too shall pass

When The Phone Rings

My heart doesn't need to see you
Just as it doesn't forget to beat
If by tomorrow either one
Of these things changes
I won't need to explain this

You are my light
Like the lens in my eye
Captured an image of you
Holding it between my nerves
Shooting fireworks in my veins

You are my walk
In a straight line
Time will take the doors between us
one by one
Year by year

You are my pen
Writing ink on my skin
Like my fingertips again
On the contours of your smile

I will kiss the frowns
Like they were old friends
Who visited us for tea

I will fold you into me
Like beach towels on holidays

I will take you now
In my dreams
Till I wake and you're there
With me

Remembering now
Like a song we both
Loved on the radio

Window View

Where scratch cards lay like graves marked hope
rubbish line the streets in gutters
people stand at ATMs
Fiddling with loose change
They used to file off silver strips
checking as they look over their shoulder
Maybe this time their money
Will be in
fast cars skid off curbs
where people walk
heads down
For pennies or a smoke
looking out for shapes in the dark sofa line corners
like the homeless love open plan
In their living room
While we all
Walk through with our boots on
Past their set of drawers
A kitchen stool
Like they got sick of having nothing
set their lines
For us to walk around
Leaving marks in the dirt
While we leaving our progress
In the street
Things we don't need
As we all try to move on

Just To Say

It's midnight,
I am feeling a little out of sorts,
So I wrote you a note,
Words to remind me,
I am not alone.
It's one o'clock and the feeling's not gone,
I write you a line,
How silly the mind,

As the reason I am still sitting up
At 2am is that.
The woman downstairs.
Well her washer broke.
Asked if she could use mine?
That's fine,
She chatted about her electronic problem,
The shutter would bang and click
As if someone was playing games,
I looked,
She said it didn't matter
I said please tell me
She said that a man had died in my room
She was glad it wasn't hers
She said it was five months before they knew,
The smell was the sign,
I looked in my mind for the first sign
A jolt at midnight two nights running.
The way I had to move my bed
Because something didn't feel right

Now I am sat at 4am
Looking at the door
The emergency lighting only comes on
in the landing when you walk past
It's done that twice.
So I thought I would write you a note that's turned into a letter
I know you would say I am being silly.
But as you're not here
I am writing to you,
Just to say.

Maybe

Maybe today was a good day
I woke up
When too many have not
I got my neighbour's washing done
They still haven't fixed her drum

Maybe this was a good day
I walked in to town
To save a quid
Gave it to the man under the bridge

Maybe this was a good day
I saw a beetle
Stuck in my window and I showed him the way

Maybe today was a good day.

The Journey Journal

The journal started in my mind,
I become aware of floating,
Wanting to be proactive,
Perhaps take up swimming?
Soft tissue forming,
A tender voice,
That drifted in on amniotic fluid.

The journey was quick.
My holiday.
Broke with the tide,
It was time,
To go back,
Or to go forward?
To my place.

My journey was harder than I thought,
Stops and starts.
Through unfamiliar routes,
Led me to wanting to go back.
My journey was long,
Looking forward to heading,
To new beginnings.
Living in the world,
With colour and texture.

My journey made many mistakes.
Little at first,
Like losing things around the house,
Eventually it all adds up.
My hardest journey.
Was saying goodbye,
When I didn't know it was time.
You were there and when I come back,
You were not.
How careless of me
To have forgot,
Where you place the things you love.
But not remember where they have gone.

Broken Mirrors

They said it was a phase.

Roll on the days
when this supposed craze
leaves my body
lets go of its hold over dreams
tag teams and believes
I am all I can be
with every part of my body
that my eyes only quickly dart across
in showers and broken mirrors
When this phase
no longer causes me this much pain,
binding chest to compress
the lines of me

So the lie is me?
Nothing in all this time
Is me

Past the teenage years
To my twenties mocking me still
My thirties now a joke
My forties losing hope

Why don't you see me?
Sat in waiting rooms
Names on waiting lists
Dissed on phone calls
They continue to cut me off
List me under specialist care
Is that fair?

To see me clearly
Is to define me merely
I will not be erased.

Class Divide

Born into poverty
In a play now
Pay later culture
Today is displayed on shop windows
The only way to obtain this dream is shop theft
Say you're never doing it again
But it gets easier every time
Born into society
Head's full of anxiety
Mums not good at sobriety
School's told you you're too behind
But outside it's sunny
The only activity that's free

Born into inequality
Blame the immigrants
Blame the jobcentre
Blame benefits
Blame reality
Blame the drink

Born into culture
Intergenerational prison families
The stop and search structure that's built on colour
Nature or nurture
Straight out of prison
How do I fix this?
Born into a system
That's grass roots started in slavery
That would build more prisons for public safety
That fund police rather than community centres and education
That believe longer sentences are better than rehabilitation
Born in prison
Newborns die in HMP Bronzefield and Styal
But there's no public outcry
Denied basic healthcare
Proves no one cared anyway
We're not Norway?
The system has always been this way

Education

Lost my voice through yawning
Teachers calling
My eyes are avoiding
While it's dawning on her to change her notes
'This one's a dreamer."
Then her eyes roll to meet me
Whisper under breath
While the reaper points at my answers
I would rather fake a seizure
than try to please her as she leans over my desk
'Speak to me after class.'

Left school with no heart
With a mistrust of the system that got me this far
Eyes forward fast the courtroom
Feeling like Caesar at the end of his life
Chained I was taken down the stairs to the afterlife

Years went by
Walked out into the sunshine
Like I had been inside Plato's cave
and only seen the shadows of a life
Time to rearrange the writing on the wall
Enrolled in university
So much diversity
How did I ever live in black and white?
To this anniversary
I want to thank all my teachers that got me this far

Rebuilding Trust

First published in TransVerse 2

Rebuilding trust,
That turned to dust,
More smoke in my eyes,
Then lies.
I'm telling jokes to hide my worst fears.
Yet these tears feed my demons.
Who sit in my chest banging ribs tearing at heart strings.
I'm looking in the cracks and seeing broken,
but you fill it with gold and tell me I'm the token,
The thing you've been missing
and I don't believe in miracles!
 Not since my mum died while I was still inside,
but there you stand with outreached hands.
You look at me like I'm the thunderbolt from Zeus' hand.
Like I'm the strength you needed,
yet I was never anyone's hero,
 just a villain, the Joker.
The moral to the story,
but you hold me and you tell me,
I am your ocean
and I think of all the times I was told I was worthless,
a mess of floating debris
yet you said I was your sunken treasure!
You held me in the storms I created,
In all the chaos!
You looked at me like I was the map to your lost,
the key to your door!
No matter how I mourned
the me before sin coated me in paint,
you looked at me and said I was a rainbow!
I know now what it feels like to finally breathe
with you as my Queen,
I will rebuild the trust that left me.

Destination

The story starts,
Where you choose to enter,
I lost my way,
But found redemption,
Not sure when,
Like children listening,
To nursery rhymes designed to link laurels with their morals,
What's mine?
Wagon rides on sweat,
Out of breath,
Timed dinners,
Poor discussions,
I wake up in nightmare's sweat,
To reconnect with the space,
I left,
At empty chairs at dinner tables,
In cinema queues,
On bar stools and fancy restaurants,
My family roots got broken,
The seed of stems,
Trying to regrow,
I found a way to re-pot,
Re-ponder and redirect my destination,
To separate the darkness,
In me,
To look up out of all I knew,
To move forward
To find the light.

We

You are so far,
Yet never nearer,
Tears may fall and fill wells,
Running into streams,
To something bigger,
Our love,
Born out of lock and key,
Has found freedom in me,
We will build a bridge,
So we can walk between the stars,
Our minds have had that power all along,
The sea of my thoughts,
Brave storms,
Wave after wave of chaos,
Yet you always bring the sun to my horizon,
If our reality is based upon the uncertainty principle,
Then our hearts will beat through all this,
We will be the dark energy,
As the map surrounds us,
We will walk off its frayed edges and into the universe.

Together

All that separates
Between me and you,
are the birds whose wings cut through air we share,
whose song is the same wherever it lands,
all that separates us,
are butterflies who do not mind where flowers stand,
 Your end or mine,
 my heart or ours,
its beats only fly then glide
no matter how far

Journey Through Time

I'm traveling back
In rows of seats
Were people flick through phones
Some sleep
Dipping in to conversations
I am lost in window views
Of fields: torn patches
Green, brown, black to gold
The lines cut by farmers
Horses, sheep, cows
Are no longer pictures in my mind
Time has gone
Sentence done
None of them notice the sun
Earphones connect them
I dip in and out of blurred windows
Listen to conversations
Two girls talking about family trips to Italy
She touches her face, talks about mental health
I see the Pandora ring on her finger
I linger in memories
That girl inside showing off
The same ring
sold for half a busci*
Two journeys connected by mine
Through time
Back to visit
The love I left behind

*It stands for buscipan - a drug they do inside but you can buy it in
pound shops on the outside*

My Street

We breathe out air
Walk past people
Like we don't care
Words formed but no one
Sees the stories unfold
Only written in headlines
Poverty lines graffiti and carved
Colour blind yet
our world is designed by the lies we tell ourselves
We live in dirty streets
One language drinks
One colour brutalized
Two colours criminalised
Three
We look through the lens of media
Wondering what the other sees

Blonde hair in a sea of regret
Empires built on his white face
He runs in the playground
The other boys see his difference
The only boy with no uniform
The other boys learn pain in different ways
Social, educational, economical racism
But for now they play
He climbs over the wall
Gets screamed out by the teacher
He's already squaring up
mock fighting those who cross him
the teacher continues shouting
He bows his head
kicks his scuffed trainers against gravel

She may see his white face
Like her troubles to get where she has
He may see someone else who hates him
Her face covered with a veil of religious modesty
Will she judge him the same?

What we breathe is lack of humanity
In exam halls
Prison floors
School doors
We shut one door for another to open
These streets build to contain
The school walls secure but untamed

I look from a window as he swings his warn jacket
Like I looked when I stood
In the pizza parlour
as he argued his way to the front of the queue
Jamming dirty hands in pockets
With change
Words don't match his age
 he wanted his dinner
I saw him again small pale and thin
Pedalling with a fake rev siren
I wonder as he grows
From then
 to now
 to who?
Will he stay out of prison?
Will he fight?
Will he rev real bikes
Stolen at night
Will he remember how hard it was
On all the days I crossed his path
Or was that a memory that will make him smile?

What Do You Want To Know About Prisons?

What do you want to know about prisons?
When the oldest form of punishment is death.

How far have we come?
How many deaths are saved for cells,
rather than a public courtyard?

What do you want to know about prisons?
Where religion blends in with black and white uniforms.
Reform started with the Quaker Elizabeth Fry.
Yet the Quakers' claim was solitary confinement

What do you want to know about prisons?
That the only audition needed is poverty?
No government vote on prison admissions increase
Just a vote for longer sentencing

What do you want to know about prisons?
You only get the left leg of the chicken
where you learn the definition
of 'mind your business'. A place that holds
more innocent victims and imprisons less villains
than media headlines. Where red tape
is drawn like chalk lines, competition, division,
racism and superstition. Too many pigeons
in conditions that require
a special edition of *Panorama*.

What do you want to know about prison?
Witness the crimson faces on cut visits.
Living inside is a mission. A collision
of what's missing. A tuition in how to listen
An exhibition, supervision, repetition
More wisdom written in graffiti lined on scuffed walls.
A revision of an exam we never asked for
This is Britain's definition, a preconditioned
redefinition of a Dickens-era

Reliving

As if written in my soul
Folds the pages of trying to forget
Guilt and shame like a shroud
Stained like oil weeping through my chest
I am hexed
Marked to myself
Like a medieval curse
No hell waiting to burn for me
When I made it for myself on earth
Perceptions like hexagons
Frame my world
Spinning through oblivion
My mind loses control
If penitence was enough to release this heavy coat
I would have woke up to summer's breeze
Not an angry winter with the white witch
I am stirring in this sleep
Sharing the space with you
Like a silent movie
Dreaming on repeat
To wake in lonely bitter judgement
Will you ever forgive me?
I raise my blankets like hankies
To cover my face
Listen to the rain like waves
Against my window pane
echoing in this storms swollen sounds
Is the hope one day I can forgive myself
While I have shed old skins
Wounds just grown over
Thick veins coarse caught in traps of pain
Slash them open
I am more now
Then what has been
But what hangs in between is a noose
I can't seem to repent
I rebury this time capsule and wait for my fate
Changed from my mistakes
I still wonder what could have been.

Tough On Crimes

When children live in deprivation
When they grew up with bars on windows
Doors next door are reinforced
To stop the police from smashing them in
How's longer sentences going to deter them?

When the school system divides some for prison
Society excludes those who did not fit in
When it's easier to be perceived as a drug dealer
because of the colour of your skin
Where electric scooters are used for drug deliveries
By kids who need more than the life they were given

When the quilts of those
Line shops
while others shop
Were garden trampolines sit on concrete
next to the fumes of the main road
How's 'tough on crime' going to deter
An underclass that's barely surviving?

In all my two years inside
Those prisons house those who know
Those who grow like vines on the outside of properties
Unable to access resources
Locked out like squatters
Handcuffed like intruders
Systems designed to make you stand in line
Forced to tick boxes and grovel
Then wait for council hovels
Where everyone knows their place
Where nothing seems to change
Where government limits public funding
To those who deserve
To those it's ok to hurt
In the public's best interest
Prison is the only place you can't get evicted from

Caroline

protest in prison
No funds to paint pictures
No room for banners
That's not volumetric controlled
Papers destroy people
pick up headlines
thinking they're winning
new votes and stir moral panic
Facts denied
Society alive!
Crime is big business
We need more police
Longer sentences
Control and punishment
We want retribution!

Protest in prison
Voices lost in echoes through tunnelled corridors
No staff
Self-harm is free
Paint the walls in red
Inside or out, where does the label stop
That's why it's called
Taking flack

An Ode To Solitude

They said it was attitude
That saw four walls and no room
It certainly wasn't the finger food
That left me cuckoo inside
When I got out just in time for a brew
Who knew the world would be on
Lock down
But as aloof as I sound
My CV as an ex-offender shows I'm overqualified

Lockdown

Dodge the rubbish
Avoid the debris
Society doesn't live here
Just relics of a time forgot
When more than pigeons lined the streets
A bottle of Old Peculiar sits next to a wall
We're told to isolate
Guess the writing's on the wall
What once was, is no more
Before I shut the front door
I breathe in this mortal coil

British Built

Covid in prison
Woman told it's probably flu
While made to walk to nurses
Who left behind bedside manners
For twitter highlights
 no spotlight on politicians
who use criminals
As sub-human growth
to build the economy
More votes in prisons booming
Non-human warehouses
To divide beliefs
that sub-humans exist
as criminal
Societies are the frame
Like It's the pinnacle to meet
Yet the media treat humans like they're unhuman
Watch them fight for no resources
In special edition Truman shows
That's the true crime
Time to review these cruel illusions of justice

I See Hope

This poem was selected to be printed and distributed with food parcels in East Leeds at Christmas. For POEM IN A BOX, the 6 Line Poem project, 104 poets submitted poems. 8 poems were chosen by 3 judges and in association with Leeds Chapel FM in 2020.

I see hope stenciled in graffiti
Sweetie do your jacket up it's cold
We are separated, deflated
But beneath masks
I still see illuminated smiles
wrinkle in people's eyes.

Christmas Inside

Given to chapel to put into Christmas booklet in HMP Low Newton

It's Christmas
Don't forget to social distance
Smile at those who pass you on the wings
Whether Christian, Pagan or Muslim
Practice forgiveness
Witness queerness
Don't judge
Be the change in the system
Be the voice happy to do business
In listening and kindness
Joy and love
This is Christmas
A lot of it says out of business
But we can rise above
Dance in cells
Shout up to the room above
Hope you're ok!
This is Christmas
This is Christmas
Let's pick ourselves up
Whistle a tune
Get the biscuits
Phone the missus
Write a letter
The year's mostly done
We got this
Pass it on

COVID 19

I got out in late May
Felt freedom breathe in me
Tease and knelt on green grass
Eased my way back into society
Who looked at my freedom
Like Achilles heel
My nerves felt wet under stress
To burn under flame when pressed
Icarus was not my name
I changed my mind inside
Now out I should remain
Tamed my demons
No longer did I feed them
I grew inside lockdowns and patdowns
Roll calls and StandFasts
Hours of blank walls
Days of no showers
Feed now locked in
Yet out here
The world is judging
Now society has a virus
Now I see people bored and isolated
Fighting for food
Who's to blame
Panic buyers, government warnings,
Under-staffing losing to the economic climate
Time to change
Yet the world is still divided

Lockdown Again

I live in words
Like books are the friends
I give myself
Like letters sit with me
On nights when day
Never seems to break
I go from one room to the next
Finding lost sentences
Plots that have a twist
In the pots that line my kitchen sink
Paragraphs flowing through paradise
as I daydream over coffee
Ponder breaks in text
Vexed as the neighbours bang
Between paper and page
I am cut
Isolated from the world
Locked in a book
I could be anyone

What Makes A Man

I have been walking
Talking my way through not talking
About ways to be a man
My memories retrieve notes I have made
Powerful, predator, punching, preaching
Yet I keep walking
Self talking
Changing the narrative as I change my body
Reciting lines men or boys have thrown at me
Like a fishing line
My mouth open
Caught, hung up, out in the open
Man and boy observing me
Gasping awkwardly
'Not very big, this one?'
Like my ability to be a man is questioned
by how I can crush another man?
How I can force those to walk faster once it's darker
How I stand in line
How I shout *mine's a pint*
How I look around
How I hold my ground
I walk around
Watching out and moving aside for these men
Who don't owe anyone anything
As I walk through the park
I see a man walking with his hood up
Talking on his phone like a road man
Next to him his son whispers something
He shouts: 'Be a man'
While he walks ahead
The boy keeps looking back at him as he crosses the park
Walking past
Hood up
He watches a man playing football with his son
He takes in a deep breath, stands up straight
As he heads to the playground
Alone

My Brother

When you were born
I was there
Between blue and cord and clear the room
I saw you
I heard you breathe and scream
My world had been just me for seven years
Then there was you
The first born son
I knew then that I was born a girl
The connection not made in my mind
Till I saw you
A baby boy
Strong, fierce, loud
Handed down the family names
To my disdain
My father replied but if we had done that with you
"Do you want Olive, Daisy or Maria?"
But he didn't understand
That's when I knew he never would
I felt my heartbreak like skidding on ice
When you were born
I was already seven
You made me realize I would never be alone
As long as I had you
my brother
Even as we grew
I reached out into the abyss of gender bias
Looking for my maleness and only found
'Toxic' marked on bottles
Generation after generation
Passed down to me
The first born
When you were born
I already knew more than I dared to speak
Heat would rise in my cheeks
As my parents repeat
But only little boys do this
Little girls should be…

THE BOY BEHIND THE WALL by Dalton Harrison

When you were born
I was the only one who could make you laugh
My best accomplishment so far
When we got older
When I got told more
Young boys do this
Young girls
Women
Boys and men
I looked in the mirror between all that was said
I looked at you growing not knowing
While they told you what they expected
You went from grin to rebellion
Wore your hair in a ponytail
While mine got shorter
You wore black on your nails and stood up
To our father
I hid myself, built myself
With the tools my generation had given me
Your reality was so much different
Till one day I looked at you
A man, big beard and short back and sides
You pulled me up with one hand
It's ok
My brother

Whitby

A creative exercise with Becky Cherriman for LLLC Podcast with University of Leeds

Blue skies
White streams jetting across reflecting in the sea
A world of mystery
Taste salt on my lips from running
Feel the breeze surround me like a warm embrace
I can see the edges of the horizon
Mark the space between me and my destiny
Bouncing boats
Blur and dip in front of me
The echoes of life surround me
Birds shriek
Children shout out in glee
My friends call on me
Throwing rocks as they skim
I feel the sun run down me
like a warm drink on a winter's day
I crave all that's been
As we had back to the bus for fish and chips

Another Day

The morning after she was raped
Was the first day of sun after all that rain
The birds loudly chirped
Street shadows jumped Infront of walkers
Dancing in the morning light
Cars hummed
Curtains twitched, letting in all the colours
Freshly coated electronic boxes
Stood waiting in line like dinner guests
Panting dogs dig for balls
But that was my walk

I pictured the streets in which she walked
Shattered glass like the fragments of lives
Intertwined in poverty and crime
Designed to break you
Forever change you
Where doing risk assessments
are more important than checking:
Are you really doing alright?

I look past the tears in my eyes
To white clouds
That at one time
We had both looked up at
when we were locked inside

Purple Visits

You arrive a few minutes late.
face encased in a smile when you see mine.
In the top corner, I see my eyes dilate.
In the background, officers debate.
Snaked patterns of black and white behind you.
One of my favourite officers waves as he passes,
mask hiding a 'Hi, how you doing?'
over glasses and white spiky hair.
Nothing is erased in these moments.
You and I. laughing at old jokes.
Fate never separated us at gates.
reshaped our love to fit bars and barb wire.
Dates marked on forms reserved for regime routine,
monitoring all phone calls and videos.

The riot bell goes off. Bravo wing exercise yard.
A sound that continues to make my stomach pump acid to my throat,
While you still make my heart jump hoops to find hope.
We ran out of time.
countdown from five to one.

Dreams

Dreams riding the train. Each freeze frame.
The light from the sky. The grass that took
years to find I'm breathing through a mask.
Never saw dreams change. But they did inside.
They did in time. The dreams we have when
we face the wall when we only see black
and white, grey and silver brown and rust
locks and dust, blood and distrust, lust then brushed aside.

Roughed up on self-destruct. Crushed in between
choices. Flushed hope down. Unjust as you see
the violence that leaves scars inside. Women
thrust into the system. The dreams we have
in the final hours after court rooms close.
Locked in. Never saw the colour until now.
Riding the train. Riding the train. Believing in my dreams.

University Life

I lived where sociology met urban streets and criminology
I was the biology of all I saw
Every dust-lined cover on the house where I was born
I lived in situations that created chaos
That grew out of economics
Cultural social problems was the quilt to make my bed
My history created a future of words I wanted to understand
I have walked between geography and penology
Were mythology is only defined as life to those who live inside
I hold the key to everything they want to be
A reality where the only key
is the one I use to lock my door when I go outside

I who can now be the governor of my own body
I who was once not allowed to go anywhere
without being escorted
I am now so much more than the faces
who sentenced me as if I was nothing

I am ready to start my course
in criminal justice and criminology
Ready to understand
the individual, social, legal and political forces that shape crime
I have done the practical
I have been where few students have seen
in pages of statistics
of illusions created by Netflix
I will line my shelves with the books
that shape the bodies of me and all of those I know
I will read the words that look at all the places I once thought of as
home
I will turn the page that has framed my life in a legacy that I will
change
I will reframe and know my worth
I will enter university life no longer the person who sat in a cell
Looking out at the world.

It's History, It's Poetry

I pack my old prison bag
Lined with clothes and my issue of *Catcher in the Rye*
Don't need to look back
Each house a shine to come dine with poverty
Locks old and rusting
Living door to door squalor
Needles lining the gutter
Seen my share of broken belts and blood stains
Burnt spoons thrown over the gate
When all there is hate

I count my blessings after all I have written
I count my blessings rebuilding my vision
I count my blessings while I move out of here
After four years on bail
After two years in prison
After two years on probation
After too many tears
After tests
After seeing so many get re-arrested
Return as guests to her majesty pleasure
I am the best I can be

I can't regret what I can't be
The contest is against me
The rest is history

Tempus Novo

meaning new time

I look in the mirror.
New work uniform in navy blue.
Hands that rub the fabric,
remembers dust on low brick.
The sound of bang-up.
The taste of tears like rain in the air.
Fold paper to make origami hearts,
that tear under touch.

Time has slammed enough doors.
Locked, bolted and secured.
To allow this moment now?
Guilt has unbuilt life.
The price of my reflection.
Rebuilding, remaining, reminding myself.
One day, at a time.

We Share This City

Leeds, home of football players
Home of academic measures
Where drunks like McDonald's on Sunday morning
Passing workers just dawning on a new day
Those who sleep on the streets
Lay on a fresh bed of concrete
Underneath shop windows selling tents

We share this city we share this city

With women who sit on the same floor
next to bus stops
chatting to those just woken
in sleeping bags freshly washed in the morning air
The taste of liquor makes humanity appear
Strangers become confidantes
Men call out to those with coffee
holding theirs up; *yeah, safe mate*
Dates become the possibility of more
Blurred in the memory of night
Still holding for a future over breakfast

We share this city we share this city

With those left stranded
calling out for loose change to get home
Those who are lost ask for directions
Where poverty, privilege and pride protest
Live Side by side
In a city that welcomes all, no matter their past

We share this city we share this city

This city of candyfloss vape corners
Breathe in sandalwood and oak
Like a forest once stood
Cider diners on street sidewalks
Takeout shops and restaurants

THE BOY BEHIND THE WALL by Dalton Harrison

Where graffiti marks the spot
where words meant more
now covered in silent masked lip moving screams
by the fallen on spice
dicing between the war on being misunderstood
stood leaving speech bubbles above their heads

We share this city we share this city

Shattered glass and condoms
the scene of passion or unwanted trauma
Well-fed pigeons weave
feeding to their own head-bopping tune
fighting for more
Between drunks who shout for war
Past the early morning runners
Girls shriek drunk between bites of food
You're all off to work
Have a nice day

We share this city
We share this city
We share this city

Burgess Hill

I went back to all the places you took me
Walked the roads
Round the corners running ridges with my fingers
Sat on walls you may have rested a bag on
Before I was born
I went into Uncle Sam's
Where you had my 11th birthday
Ordered milkshake
But there was no banana
Told them how far I had come
He couldn't picture it
The distance between then and now
More years then he had been on this earth
Yet here we both stand
In the place you stood
Inhabiting my memory mixed with reality
You were here with me
You were here with me
You were here with me
You are still here with me
In a body that carries me here now
My DNA like don't need to ask
My eyes reflect my brother's
who reflect his daughter's when she laughs
We are built like bricks that are lifting us higher
We are building a home for the next generation to come

Acknowledgements

Bev, from induction to losing my heart to being with you since 2017, there are no walls between our love. You have changed my life, not just by giving me the love I always craved, but by showing me there is another way to live than the life I had always accepted as my fate. Thank you. You are my soulmate.

My family: To my mum, you did more for me than I could ever see. I hope you are finally looking down and smiling at me. To my brother, you have been my rock, my hand to pull me up. Thank you to my Dutch family.

My friends, especially Carla, you were my first friend inside, and what would I have done without you? My bestie, my protector, my book buddy and confidante.

Harleigh, you are funny, loyal, kind, a great listener and always there for me. I am so lucky.

Kath, my writing and creative mastermind, another thank you for taking the photo for the front cover,

Phoenix, who would have thought - from listening to gym orderly to gardens, we keep on going!

Amy, from serving my food to me in prison to being in Standfast play *High Risk*, you have come so far; a big thank you for taking my author photo for this book.

Faith Buckley, you gave me faith when no one wanted coffee with someone who had been in prison; your poetry and nature-inspired me and the adventure were gangsta.

Tracy, you have been on my PHE journey to my criminal justice and criminology degree first day. I am so happy we became friends - partners in crime! Academically speaking!

Anne L, you were the maths mentor I needed, the first person to get me to remember my lines and someone I admired for so many reasons. I miss you.

Sam, you walked with me into town; you got me to Jobcentre appointments and took me to my first museum on realise. I know wherever you are, it must be heaven. Your soul is finally free. The bag you took me to buy when I got out took me to my first day of university. I hope you find peace.

Stephanie Hirst, thank you for coming out when I could not find the words. You gave me your story and stopped me from ending mine.

Erwin James, your books kept me going inside, your outlook kept me focused on overcoming and succeeding.

LJ Flanders, you completely blew me away reading in cell work out inside and made me focus on my goals.

The officers and staff: Miss Bainbridge, you were a bright light to others, the first I met that made me smile, you would sing in the morning, 'alllllll reeeeeet!' You will never be forgotten. Fly high. True legend. Thank you for all you did. Mr Laddie, my personal officer; the prison needs more blokes like you. Mr and Mrs Bean, Miss Armitage you are a legend, you cared. You did a job that was never rewarded; thank you is not enough. Mr Elliot; thank you for supporting me at my mum's funeral and having that talk to me, Mr Briggs, you always asked if I was ok when no one bothered, you are a damn good officer, Mr P, Miss corks, Mr Mack, Miss Leckie, Miss Kitching, Robo, Miss Bartley-Swan, Mr Tennick, Miss Stockdale, Mrs Richardson, Miss Dilks, Miss Phillippo, Mr Goodall, Miss Hood, Mr Dent and Sarah, Mr Andrew White from my Buddhism group, Lisa from the Pagan side, Zoe, Gillian (when my lack of maths skills made my life so hard you were the only teacher who could make me do it; getting my Level 2 was an achievement, thank you!), Miss M. Barker, Mr Wilson, Miss Staton, Mrs Smallman Sr, Miss Smallman Jr, Miss Montgomery, Mr and Mrs Dinning, Miss Barnaby, Mr Fisher, Miss Fisk, Mr Appleby, Miss Guthers, Miss Hennessy, Miss Hicks, Mrs P, Miss Burns, Mrs Burrows, Miss Smillie, Mr Garbutt, Miss Denton, Miss Skinner and Miss B. Roberts, Liam mental health team, Gabrielle Lee. Jackie and the librarians who always listened and read my poetry! You should start up your own group! I miss you and the haven you created.

Special message: Miss Firth went above and beyond her job, and still does to this day, in Safer Custody. Her work supporting others is why I still believe there is so much humanity within the prison system, thanks to some staff - the true hidden heroes.

Jane from the Jobcentre: thank you for not sanctioning me when I missed that appointment when I thought I would get recalled as I had signed paperwork without permission from probation. I was so scared of being homeless, but you never once doubted me, and I wish there were a million of you working and supporting ex-offenders who don't understand how to access websites and fill forms online. You knew I was running on outdated rules and always had a smile and helped me so much! Not forgetting Chris, you carried on after Jane and followed her example by bringing humanity to a job that can often lead to red tape and unhappy people.

The Inside-Out programme: Dr Kate O'Brien and Dr Hannah King, Dr Josephine Phillips. Professor Fiona Measham.

Dr Kelly Henderson and Just Pips who came in to talk to us

Samaritans: Elaine, Joanne, Sandra, Beryl, posh Pat, Linda, Alan, Mr Robert Allfree - I will never forget your talk.

Think like a Scientist, Dr Phil Heron and Prof Danielle George for talking to us.

Notable mentions are Ripon House Pam; every time I wrote a poem, you said you wanted a signed copy when I published my own book, and I used to laugh at you, having only been out of prison for three weeks, I never dreamed it would happen. I still cannot believe how all the things you told me to do in those three months have become real. Thank you to Emma, the manager and Mary, Becky, Gail, Jenni, Fiona, Donna, Christine, Vinny and Jackie.

My writing tutors are Gill Lambert, Becky Cherriman, Amanda Dalton and Mary Colson. Victoria Fayne, what would I have done without you in lockdown? You are incredible.

Peter Spafford and Chapel FM

Chaucer Cameron, you inspire me.

Phil Pearce from Life Experience - what you do for so many people goes unheard, but what you did for me is beyond words. Thank you.

Stepth's place for the activism and the blogs we make quite the team!

Honorary StandFast members Lily Procella, Faith Buckley and Sophie Macwannell. Mim Skinner, you donated a laptop that wrote this book - you are a queen of hearts outside in the community. Your humanity has changed lives: where you find red tape, you find another way. Thank you. Gareth Smiles, you are so talented and changing my poetry into art was enough to make my eyes water.

Fiona Chapel, Lynne Cade, and Paul Devlin from The University of Leeds, you are the most incredible people and teachers. Thank you.

Prisoners Education Trust: the community and care you provide is not only a culture of education and growth, but empathy and a chance to evolve. I cannot thank you enough! If this is the first four years, I cannot wait for the future.

Tempus Novo Kath and Fiona, what a dream team! Your support and encouragement have been amazing.

Nepacs and Junction 42, keep doing what you're doing!

Opera North, you are a force: you brought music, theatre and opera into my life and I never looked back.

When I went to my first poetry event, after learning that poetry events happen outside when I did my arts and languages access course with the Open University funded by Prisoners Education Trust, I first heard the name Ash Brockwell who had published *TransVerse*. I thought, 'If he ever does another, I am going to be in it!' I was. But I never dreamed Ash would give me my lifelong dream of my own book - this dream that I had at ten, finding a poetry book my mum had published the year before I was born. Ash, you believed in me when prison poetry is seen as niche and trans narratives are only talked about negatively in the media. There is no 'thank you' big enough.

In memory of all the women now gone. To the women I argued with, laughed with, talked to and listened to. The women who I walked past ate alongside and stood in lines with—the women who walked in groups in yards with no grass or hope. You were valid. You are remembered. I am sorry it wasn't enough. I hope you find your freedom.

Further Reading

Books

- **Captive Genders: Trans Embodiment and the Prison Industrial Complex - Second Edition**
  https://smile.amazon.co.uk/dp/1849352348/ref=cm_sw_r_apan_glt_fabc_4ZQG6RN1AJHCR26XV8FM
- O'Brien, K., Hobbs, D. & Westmarland, L. (2008). **Negotiating Violence and Gender: Security and the Night Time Economy in the UK**. In Violence in Europe: Historical and Contemporary Perspectives. Body-Gendrot, S. & Spierenburg, P. Springer. 161-176.
- O'Brien, K., Meahsam, F. & King, H. (2017). **University students and prisoners learning collaboratively**. In Life Beyond Crime. Crane, P. Lemos Crane.
- **Criminal Women (1985): Criminal Women: Autobiographical Accounts (Feminist perspectives):** Amazon.co.uk: Carlen, Pat: 9780745600888
- **Criminal Women:** Gender Matters
  https://www.amazon.co.uk/Criminal-Women-Matters-Maggie-ONeill/dp/1529208416
- **Living with the Dominator: A book about the Freedom Programme:** https://www.amazon.co.uk/Living-Dominator-About-Freedom-Programme/dp/0955882702

Websites for Further Information and Support Links

- https://blogs.egu.eu/geolog/2019/05/29/bringing-geoscience-into-prisons/
- King, Hannah (2016). The Connection between Personal Traumas and Educational Exclusion in
- Young People's Lives. Young 24(4): 342-358.
- Hobbs, D., O'Brien, K & Westmarland, L. (2007). Connecting the Gendered Door: Women,
- Violence and Doorwork. British Journal of Sociology 58(1): 21-38.

- King, H., Measham, F. & O'Brien, K. (2019). Building Bridges Across Diversity: Utilising the Inside-Out Prison Exchange Programme to promote an egalitarian higher education community within three UK prisons. International Journal of Bias, Identity and Diversity in Education 4(1): 66-81.
- The European Journal of criminology https://journals.sagepub.com/home/euc
- The transgender pains of imprisonment, Matthew Maycock https://doi.org/10.1177%2F1477370820984488
- Fair Play to Women, Transgender and Crime. https://www.stephsplace.uk/fair-play-to-women-and-transgender-crime.cfm
- http://www.prisonreformtrust.org.uk/
- https://www.prisonerseducation.org.uk/
- https://www.aurorand.org.uk/
- https://beyondthestreets.org.uk/
- https://niaendingviolence.org.uk/
- https://one25.org.uk/

Transgender further readings

- The Phallus Palace - Dean Kotula
- FTM: Female to Male Transsexuals in Society - Aaron Devor (older editions by Holly Devor)
- Gender Bending - Aaron Devor
- Jamison Green - Becoming a Visible Man
- Michael nee Laura - Liz Hodgkinson
- Stone Butch Blues - Leslie Feinberg (novel, available as downloadable pdf)
- Nina Here Nor There (My Journey Beyond Gender) - Nick Krieger
- The Testosterone Files - Max Wolf Valerio
- Transmen and FTMs - Jason Cromwell
- So Different - Peter Stirling
- Raising Ryland - Hillary Whittington
- Hung Jury - Trysten T. Cotton
- Self-Made Men - Henry Rubin
- The Last Time I Wore a Dress - Daphne Scholinski (now Dylan Scholinski)
- The First Man-Made Man - Pagan Kennedy
- Bumbling into Body Hair - Everett Maroon
- Paralian - Liam Klenk
- Out of the Ordinary - Michael Dillon aka Lobsang Jivaka
- The Making of a Man - Maxim Februari
- Dear Sir or Madam - Mark Rees
- A Self-Made Man - Paul Hewitt
- As Nature Made Him: The Boy who was Raised as a Girl - John Colapinto
- The Boy who was Born a Girl - Jon and Luisa Edwards
- But For the Grace - Robert Allen
- From the Inside Out: Radical Gender Transformation, FTM and Beyond - Morty Diamond
- My Breasts, My Choice: Journeys through Surgery - ed. by Brown, Aslin & Carey (some chapters by trans men)

Some further articles, videos and issues spoken about by Dalton Harrison and Standfast a collective founded by Dalton to help explore issues within the Justice system through creativity.

- Samaritan https://youtu.be/01YcKyBhwkw
- Opera north https://youtu.be/YTZvJ1nUmk8
- https://artstogetherleeds.co.uk/partner/standfast-productions/
- Www.Standfast.uk
- https://www.chapelfm.co.uk/elfm-player/shows/list/writing-on-air-2021-festival-part-2/
- The Debate Continues https://www.stephsplace.uk/the-debate-continues-by-dalton-harrison.cfm
- https://metro.co.uk/2020/02/26/education-prison-changed-life-every-prisoner-deserves-
- opportunity-12306294/?ito=article.amp.share.top
- https://www.prisonerseducation.org.uk/2019/07/roots-to-stem-bringing-science-education-to-
- prisons/
- https://www.pinknews.co.uk/2020/11/02/trans-prison-system-prisoners-dalton-harrison-
- transgender-man-transition-crime/
- Transgender – special treatment? https://insidetime.org/transgender-special-treatment/
- Dalton's story: "I felt like someone believed in me" - Prisoners' Education Trust
- https://www.prisonerseducation.org.uk/2021/10/pet-launch-new-strategy-read-daltons-foreword/
- Dalton Harrison: I was in Prison https://www.stephsplace.uk/dalton-harrison-i-was-in-prison.cfm
- Smashing it September https://www.stephsplace.uk/smashing-it-in-september.fm

LGBTQ+ online resources

- https://youtube.com/ashleymardell

My Genderation

- https://youtu.be/7iIlBBbMI98
- https://aydiandowling.com/
- https://transleeds.org/

Also published by Reconnecting Rainbows:

TransVerse, We Won't Be Erased! Poems and Song Lyrics by Transgender and Non-Binary Writers
Edited by Ash Brockwell, 2019

TransVerse II, No Time For Silence: Words of Survival, Resilience and Hope
Edited by Ash Brockwell, 2021

Forthcoming

TransVerse III, Transcendence: Words of Faith, Love and Authenticity

TransVerse IV, The Wait Is Killing Us: The UK Trans Healthcare Crisis In Our Own Words

Songs of Remembering: Singing Ourselves Back Together in a Broken World

Message to you, the reader

By Dr Ash Brockwell, co-founder of Reconnecting Rainbows

You are enough.
You are valid
You are loved.

Your voice matters.
Your story matters.
Your words matter.

Write it.
Speak it.
Sing it.

Never give up.

THE BOY BEHIND THE WALL by Dalton Harrison

9 781838 342524